THE
DISPLACED

THE
DISPLACED

REFUGEE WRITERS ON
REFUGEE LIVES

EDITED BY
VIET THANH NGUYEN
PULITZER PRIZE–WINNING AUTHOR OF *THE SYMPATHIZER*

ABRAMS PRESS, NEW YORK

A version of "Flesh and Sand" previously appeared in the November 2017 issue of *Vogue Italia*.

A version of "How Succulent Food Defeated Trump's Wall Before It Has Been Built" previously appeared in the *Los Angeles Times*, and is also published in his essay collection, *Homeland Security Ate My Speech*.

"The Ungrateful Refugee" previously appeared in the *Guardian*.

Abrams Books will donate 7.5% of the cover price of this book to the International Rescue Committee (IRC) with a minimum contribution of $25,000. The IRC, a not-for-profit organization, is dedicated to providing humanitarian aid, relief and resettlement to refugees and other victims of oppression or violent conflict. Please refer to the back of this book for more information about the IRC.

Library of Congress Control Number: 2018963575

ISBN: 978-1-4197-3511-0
eISBN: 978-1-68335-207-5

Printed and bound in the United States
10 9 8 7 6 5

Abrams books are available at special discounts when purchased in quantity for premiums and promotions as well as fundraising or educational use. Special editions can also be created to specification. For details, contact specialsales@abramsbooks.com or the address below.

ABRAMS The Art of Books
195 Broadway, New York, NY 10007
abramsbooks.com

Contents

11 Introduction
VIET THANH NGUYEN

23 The Road
CHRIS ABANI

31 Last, First, Middle
JOSEPH AZAM

43 Common Story
DAVID BEZMOZGIS

51 Flesh and Sand
FATIMA BHUTTO

61 Perspective and What Gets Lost
THI BUI

67 How Succulent Food Defeated
Trump's Wall Before It Has Been Built
ARIEL DORFMAN

75 Guests of the Holy Roman Empress
Maria Theresa
LEV GOLINKIN

81 The Parent Who Stays
REYNA GRANDE

91 To Walk in Their Shoes
MERON HADERO

99 God's Fate
ALEKSANDAR HEMON

113 Second Country
JOSEPH KERTES

121 13 Ways of Being an Immigrant
POROCHISTA KHAKPOUR

129 Refugees and Exiles
MARINA LEWYCKA

137 This Is What the Journey Does
MAAZA MENGISTE

145 The Ungrateful Refugee
DINA NAYERI

159 Am I a Refugee?
RAJA SHEHADEH

165 A Refugee Again
VU TRAN

173 New Lands, New Selves
NOVUYO ROSA TSHUMA

189 Refugee Children: The Yang Warriors
KAO KALIA YANG

197 List of Contributors

Introduction

VIET THANH NGUYEN

I was once a refugee, although no one would mistake me for being a refugee now. Because of this, I insist on being called a refugee, since the temptation to pretend that I am not a refugee is strong. It would be so much easier to call myself an immigrant, to pass myself off as belonging to a category of migratory humanity that is less controversial, less demanding, and less threatening than the refugee.

I was born a citizen and a human being. At four years of age I became something less than human, at least in the eyes of those who do not think of refugees as being human. The month was March, the year 1975, when the northern communist army captured my hometown of Ban Me Thuot in its final invasion of the Republic of Vietnam, a country that no longer exists except in the imagination of its global refugee diaspora of several million people, a country that most of the world remembers as South Vietnam.

Looking back, I remember nothing of the experience that turned me into a refugee. It begins with my mother making a life-and-death decision on her own. My father was in Saigon, and the lines of communication were cut. I do not remember my mother fleeing our hometown with my ten-year-old brother and me, leaving behind our sixteen-year-old adopted sister to guard the family property. I do not remember my sister, who my parents would not see again for nearly twenty years, who I would not see again for nearly thirty years.

My brother remembers dead paratroopers hanging from the trees on our route, although I do not. I also do not remember whether I walked the entire one hundred eighty-four kilometers to Nha Trang, or whether my mother carried me, or whether we might have managed to get a ride on the cars, trucks, carts, motorbikes, and bicycles crowding the road. Perhaps she does remember but I never asked about the exodus, or about the tens of thousands of civilian refugees and fleeing soldiers, or the desperate scramble to get on a boat in Nha Trang, or some of the soldiers shooting some of the civilians to clear their way to boats, as I would read later in accounts of this time.

I do not remember finding my father in Saigon, or how we waited for another month until the communist army came to the city's borders, or how we tried to get into the airport, and then into the American embassy, and then finally somehow fought our way through the crowds at the docks to reach a boat, or how my father became separated from us but decided to get on a boat by himself anyway, and how my mother decided the same thing, or how we eventually were reunited on a larger ship. I do remember that we were incredibly fortunate, finding our way out of the country, as so many millions did not, and not losing anyone, as so many thousands did. No one, except my sister.

For most of my life, I did remember soldiers on our boat firing onto a smaller boat full of refugees that was trying to approach. But when I mentioned it to my older brother many years later, he said the shooting never happened.

I do not remember many things, and for all those things I do not remember, I am grateful, because the things I do remember hurt me enough. My memory begins after our stops at a chain of American military bases in the Philippines, Guam, and finally Pennsylvania. To leave the refugee camp in Pennsylvania, the Vietnamese refugees needed American sponsors. One sponsor took my parents, another took my brother, a third took me.

For most of my life, I tried not to remember this moment except to note it in a factual way, as something that happened to us but left no damage, but that is not true. As a writer and a father of a son who is four years old, the same age I was when I became a refugee, I have to remember, or sometimes imagine, not just what happened, but what was felt. I have to imagine what it was like for a father and a mother to have their children taken away from them. I have to imagine what it was that I experienced, although I do remember being taken by my sponsor to visit my parents and howling at being taken back.

I remember being reunited with my parents after a few months and the snow and the cold and my mother disappearing from our lives for a period of time I cannot recall and for reasons I could not understand, and knowing vaguely that it had something to do with the trauma of losing her country, her family, her property, her security, maybe her self. In remembering this, I know that I am also foreshadowing the worst of what the future would hold, of what would happen to her in the decades to come. Despite her short absence, or maybe her long one, I remember enjoying life in Harrisburg, Pennsylvania, because children can enjoy things that adults cannot so long as they can play, and I remember a sofa sitting in our backyard and neighborhood children stealing our Halloween candy and my enraged brother taking me home before venturing out by himself to recover what had been taken from us.

I remember moving to San Jose, California, in 1978 and my parents opening the second Vietnamese grocery store in the city and I remember the phone call on Christmas Eve that my brother took, informing him that my parents had been shot in an armed robbery, and I remember that it was not that bad, just flesh wounds, they were back at work not long after, and I remember that the only people who wanted to open businesses in depressed downtown San Jose were the Vietnamese refugees, and I remember walking down the street from my parents' store and seeing a sign in a store window that said ANOTHER AMERICAN DRIVEN OUT OF BUSINESS BY THE VIETNAMESE, and I remember the gunman who followed us to our home and knocked on our door and pointed a gun in all our faces and how my mother saved us by running past him and out onto the sidewalk, but I do not remember the two policemen shot to death in front of my parents' store because I had gone away to college by that time and my parents did not want to call me and worry me.

I remember all these things because if I did not remember them and write them down then perhaps they would all disappear, as all those Vietnamese businesses have vanished, because after they had helped to revitalize the downtown that no one else cared to invest in, the city of San Jose realized that downtown could be so much better than what it was and forced all those businesses to sell their property and if you visit downtown San Jose today you will see a massive, gleaming, new city hall that symbolizes the wealth of a Silicon Valley that had barely begun to exist in 1978 but you will not see my parents' store, which was across the street from the new city hall. What you will see instead is a parking lot with a few cars in it because the city thought that the view of an empty parking lot from the windows and foyer of city hall was more attractive than the view of a mom-and-pop Vietnamese grocery store catering to refugees.

As refugees, not just once but twice, having fled from north to south in 1954 when their country was divided, my parents experienced the usual dilemma of anyone classified as an *other*. The other exists in contradiction, or perhaps in paradox, being either invisible or hypervisible, but rarely just visible. Most of the time we do not see the other or see right through them, whoever the other may be to us, since each of us—even if we are seen as others by some—have our own others. When we do see the other, the other is not truly human to us, by very definition of being an other, but is instead a stereotype, a joke, or a horror. In the case of the Vietnamese refugees in America, we embodied the specter of the Asian come to either serve or to threaten.

Invisible and hypervisible, refugees are ignored and forgotten by those who are not refugees until they turn into a menace. Refugees, like all others, are unseen until they are seen everywhere, threatening to overwhelm our borders, invade our cultures, rape our women, threaten our children, destroy our economies. We who do the ignoring and forgetting oftentimes do not perceive it to be violence, because we do not know we do it. But sometimes we deliberately ignore and forget others. When we do, we are surely aware we are inflicting violence, whether that is on the schoolyard as children or at the level of the nation. When those others fight back by demanding to be seen and heard—as refugees sometimes do—they can appear to us like threatening ghosts whose fates we ourselves have caused and denied. No wonder we do not wish to see them.

When I say *we*, I mean even those who were once refugees. There are some former refugees who are comfortable in their invisibility, in the safety of their new citizenship, who look at today's hypervisible refugees and say, "No more." These former refugees think they were the good refugees, the special refugees, when in all likelihood they were simply the lucky ones, the refugees whose fates aligned with the politics of the host country. The Vietnamese refugees who came to the United States were lucky in receiving an American charity that was born out of American guilt about the war, and resulted from an American desire to show that a capitalist and democratic country was a much better home than the newly communist country the refugees were fleeing. Cuban refugees of the 1970s and 1980s benefitted from a similar American politics, but Haitian refugees of the time did not. Their blackness hindered them, just as being Muslim hurts many Syrian refugees today as they seek refuge.

From everything I remember and do not remember, I believe in my human kinship to Syrian refugees and to those 65.6 million people that the United Nations classifies as displaced people. Of these, 40.3 million are internally displaced people, forced to move within their own countries; 22.5 million are refugees fleeing unrest in their countries; 2.8 million are asylum seekers. If these 65.6 million people were their own country, their nation would be the twenty-first largest in the world, smaller than Thailand but bigger than France. And yet, they are not their own country. They are instead—to paraphrase the art historian Robert Storr, who was writing about the role that Vietnamese people played in the American mind—the displaced persons of the world's conscience.

These displaced persons are mostly unwanted where they fled from; unwanted where they are, in refugee camps; and unwanted where they want to go. They have fled under arduous conditions; they have lost friends, family members, homes, and countries; they are detained in refugee camps in often subhuman conditions, with no clear end to the stay and no definitive exit; they are often threatened with deportation to their countries of origin; and they will likely be unremembered, which is where the work of writers becomes important, especially writers who are refugees or have been refugees—if such a distinction can be drawn.

The United Nations says that refugees stop being refugees when they find a new and permanent home. It has been a long time since I have been a refugee in the definition of the United Nations: "someone who has been forced to flee his or her country because of persecution, war, or violence." But I keep my tattered memories of being a refugee close to me. I cultivate that feeling of what it was to be a refugee, because a writer is supposed to go where it hurts, and because a writer needs to know what it feels like to be an other. A writer's work is impossible if he or she cannot conjure up the lives of others, and only through such acts of memory, imagination, and empathy can we grow our capacity to feel for others.

Many writers, perhaps most writers or even all writers, are people who do not feel completely at home. They are used to being people who are out of place, who are emotionally or psychically or socially displaced to one degree or another, at one time or another. Or perhaps that is just me. But I cannot help but suspect that it is from this displacement that writers come into being, and why so many writers have sympathy and empathy for those who are displaced in one way or another, whether it is the lonely social misfit or whether it is the millions rendered homeless by forces beyond their control. In my case, I remember my displacement so that I can feel for those now displaced. I remember the injustice of displacement so that I can imagine my writing as attempting to perform some justice for those compelled to move.

What is unjust about the lives of refugees, of stateless people, of asylum seekers, of all those who are no longer at home? When it comes to justice, it does not matter whether those in a host country think they have no obligation to refugees. Keeping people in a refugee camp is punishing people who have committed no crime except trying to save their own lives and the lives of their loved ones. The refugee camp belongs to the same inhuman family as the internment camp, the concentration camp, the death camp. The camp is the place where we keep those who we do not see as fully being human, and if we do not actively seek their death in most cases, we also often do not actively seek to restore many of them to the life that they had before, the life we have ourselves.

We should remember that justice is not the same as law. Many laws say that borders are sacrosanct, and that crossing borders without permission is a crime. Unpermitted migrants are thus criminals and the refugee camp is a kind of prison. But if borders are legal, are they also just? Our notions of borders have shifted over the centuries, just as our notions of justice and humanity have. Today we can usually move freely between cities within a country, even if those cities were once their own entities with their own borders and had fought wars with each other. Now we look back on those times of city-states—if we remember them—and I doubt few of us would want to return to such a condition.

Likewise, we should look at our current condition of national borders and we should imagine a more just world where these borders would be markers of culture and identity, valuable but easily crossed, rather than legal borders designed to keep our national identities rigid and ready for conflict and war, separating us from others. The dissolution of borders is the utopian vision of cosmopolitanism, of global peace and of a global place where no one is displaced, of humanity as a global community that is allowed its cultural differences but not the kind of differences that lead us to exploit, punish, or kill. Making borders permeable, we bring ourselves closer to others, and others closer to us. I find such a prospect exhilarating, but some find this proximity unimaginably terrifying.

If this global community has not been achieved, it is not because it is a wholly utopian fantasy, a nowhere not marked by any boundary. There have been moments in our history—and many times in our writings and our folklores and our theologies—where we have achieved the best of ourselves in our ability to welcome the other, to clothe the stranger, to feed the hungry, to open our homes. This is what we need to remember as we hope and work for a future where borders do not matter, but people do. This is the kind of memory, the memory of our own humanity, and our inhumanity, that writers can offer.

We need stories to give voice to a writer's vision, but also, possibly, to speak for the voiceless. This yearning to hear the voiceless is a powerful rhetoric but also potentially a dangerous one if it prevents us from doing more than listening to a story or reading a book. Just because we have listened to that story or read that book does not mean that anything has changed for the voiceless. Readers and writers should not deceive themselves that literature changes the world. Literature changes the world of readers and writers, but literature does not change the world until people get out of their chairs, go out in the world, and do something to transform the conditions of which the literature speaks. Otherwise literature will just be a fetish for readers and writers, allowing them to think that they are hearing the voiceless when they are really only hearing the writer's individual voice.

The problem here is that the people we call voiceless often-times are not actually voiceless. Many of the voiceless are actually talking all the time. They are loud, if you get close enough to hear them, if you are capable of listening, if you are aware of what you cannot hear. The problem is that much of the world does not want to hear the voiceless or cannot hear them. True justice is creating a world of social, economic, cultural, and political opportunities that would allow all these voiceless to tell their stories and be heard, rather than be dependent on a writer or a representative of some kind. Without such justice, there will be no end to the waves of the displaced, to the creation of ever more voiceless people, or, more accurately, to the ongoing silencing of millions of voices. True justice will be when we no longer need a voice for the voiceless.

In the meantime, we have this book of powerful voices, from writers who were themselves refugees. Joseph Azam, from Afghanistan, speaks of the long process of self-transformation that led to the shaping of his name into a more American fashion. David Bezmozgis, from the Soviet Union, settled in Canada, where he describes practicing quiet solidarity with a new refugee trying to gain permission to stay. Fatima Bhutto, born in Afghanistan to a Pakistani father from an important political lineage, submits herself to a virtual reality version of refugee experiences, and finds herself unexpectedly moved. Thi Bui, who fled the Vietnam War to come to the United States, considers the baggage and fragments of refugee life through sharply drawn pictures. Ariel Dorfman left Chile and settled in North Carolina, where he spurns the politics of Donald Trump and finds hope in a pan–Latin American supermarket. Reyna Grande, who came to America as an undocumented migrant from Mexico, raises the critical question of definitions: What makes someone a refugee versus a migrant?

Lev Golinkin, a Soviet Jewish refugee who winds up in Vienna, describes the quotidian struggle to retain humanity as the refugee experience turns one into a ghost. Meron Hadero, who came as an infant to Germany from Ethiopia, returns to Germany as an adult in order to reclaim the experiences of displacement and migration that she does not remember.

Aleksandar Hemon, a Chicagoan from Bosnia, recounts the Candide-like experiences of a fellow Bosnian who had the misfortune to live an epic life. Joseph Kertes, a Jewish refugee from Hungary, describes the unique status of Canada as a country of outsiders, next to but not quite like the United States (in a good way). Porochista Khakpour offers a precise autobiography of her journey from Iran to America, including the precarious status of being Muslim, brown, and American during a time of war. Marina Lewycka, born in a "displaced persons" camp to Ukrainian parents, settled in the UK and to a comfortable English identity—until rising anti-immigrant feeling made her question that identity. Maaza Mengiste, an American writer from Ethiopia, finds herself in an Italian café, watching an afflicted young black migrant through the window, and feeling the pain of her connection to him and so many others forced to move.

Dina Nayeri, born in Iran, raised in America, and now a UK resident, challenges the widely held idea that refugees must be grateful by showing how gratitude is a trap. Vu Tran, a Vietnamese refugee who came to Oklahoma, offers a taxonomy of the refugee's many guises: orphan, actor, ghost. Novuyo Rosa Tshuma, whose family left Zimbabwe for a South Africa that was both hospitable and hostile, describes the refugee's fear of persecution as leading to a desire to be exceptional, and hence acceptable. Kao Kalia Yang, a Hmong refugee whose family came from Laos to Minnesota, dwells on the memory of how the refugee children in her camp struggled and fought to survive.

All of these writers are inevitably drawn to the memories of their own past and of their families. To become a refugee is to know, inevitably, that the past is not only marked by the passage of time, but by loss—the loss of loved ones, of countries, of identities, of selves. We want to give voice to all those losses that would otherwise remain unheard except by us and those near and dear to us. In my case, I remember the losses of my parents, and I remember their voices. I remember the voices of all the Vietnamese refugees that I encountered in my youth, hoarse from telling their stories over and over again. But I do not remember my sister's voice. I do not remember the voices of all the refugees who shared the exodus with me and did not make it, or did not survive. But I can imagine them, and if I can imagine them, then maybe I can hear them. That is a writer's dream, that if only we can hear these people that no one else wants to hear, then perhaps we can make you hear them, too.

The Road

CHRIS ABANI

In the beginning there was a river.
The river became a road
and the road branched out to the
whole world. And
because the road was once a river
it was always hungry.

BEN OKRI, *The Famished Road*

My walk by the lake, this cold morning, is magical with wisps of mist curling away into nothing and the silent patrol of several sea birds in formation, like nature's coastguard. Back home I make a pot of Earl Grey tea for the work ahead. The hot tea also mists and the bergamot oil smell warms me, creating an old sense of comfort and safety. At my desk, in the photograph I'm looking at, a young boy of maybe ten or twelve, is carrying another younger boy. They are walking down a rural dirt road, dense bush on either side. In the distance, ahead of them, four teenage girls walk abreast, straddling the road. One has her head turned back to check up on the boys.

It is a simple photograph, elegant in its framing, smart in its depth of field, but still a simple scene: six African children walking down a rural dirt road. There is no immediate danger visible, although there is an air of tension around the boys, but still nothing to throw up any red flags. And yet I am arrested immediately, a nervousness has entered my breathing, and I am at once focused and distracted. This is despite the fact that this photograph, by Nigerian artist Victor Ekpuk, has just popped up in my Instagram feed.

Something about it is at once familiar and yet disturbing, a strange uncanny valley phenomenon. Again, this is despite the fact that I cannot know the scene, I cannot know anyone in this photograph, I cannot possibly know this place. Why? Because it was taken a few days ago, taken in fact in Surinam. And yet it has this disturbing effect, this displacement from time, from place, and even from memory. And then it dawns on me, my mind has connected this photograph to an image in my mind. And I say "image," although in the strict sense of the visual it cannot be, and the reasons for this will become clear. The image is of my elder brother Mark, barely eight, carrying my six-month-old self as we flee our home in rural Afikpo, just hours before the encroaching Nigerian Army enters our town from Ndibe Beach, where they have just landed, a mere three miles away. Not an image in the strictest sense because while I may actually remember the event deep down in a part of my consciousness, while it is possible for memory like this to be recorded indelibly even at such a young age, my ability to access it might be up for debate. I cannot have "seen" something that I was participating in. We cannot, we are told, be both in a "scene" and simultaneously "see" that scene from outside it. So, what I'm really recalling, while no less clear in every sense as the photograph I'm looking at, cannot be real. And yet it happened. This is fact.

And here we encounter in one moment some of the hardest

things about the refugee experience—that being a refugee is neither a noun nor a verb, but a stutter in time-space, always repeating. You are simultaneously always a refugee even when you are no longer a refugee. Once marked you always carry this existential "smell" of displacement. You realize that although you have lived through and always carry it with you, the experience doesn't always correlate with what feels real or what is even true to memory. So, you're always left with the annoying aftertaste of this particular trauma and its repetitive wounding without the necessary words to convey the experience. As details shift in telling and retelling you doubt your own experience of it. What is yours, what belongs to your family's recollection, what belongs to the media of the time, what belongs to what you have revisited, becomes unclear.

Have you noticed that the quintessential image for the refugee, the photographs we have come to identify with the condition always has the refugee in flight? The refugee is always on the road somewhere, on a boat somewhere, on a plane somewhere, on a train somewhere, never ever arriving. Some are carrying umbrellas, bags, children, some even have coffins strapped to the back of bicycles, sewing machines, things, on heads, in carts, on bicycles, a long thick stream of people, a human river of desperation.

There is the home that is lost and the home that can never be remade or reclaimed. You are always traveling, unable to return and unable to truly settle or belong anywhere else. Geography is not a real factor here, beyond the idea and fact of journey.

My refugee experience was as a result of the Nigerian-Biafran Civil War of 1967 to 1970. As an Igbo, the so-called rebel ethnicity, even after the war was over, even after the "No Victor, No Vanquished" speech of the then Nigerian Head of State, General Yakubu Gowon, the Igbos till this day remain kind-of-refugees even in their ancestral lands. The war is always the specter and will always be the specter haunting them. There is something about the way that refugees, more than any other kind of displaced peoples, haunt the assurances of stability that modern statehood aspires to. Perhaps because this body is proof that we have advanced much less in our "humanness," than we would like to believe.

Perhaps no other body causes as much unease as the body of the refugee. Refugees generate complex anxieties wherever in the world they go, wherever they try to resettle. I don't think this is simply the result of native fears of being overrun by a horde of refugee barbarians. It may be partly a result of guilt—most nations who take in refugees are often morally obligated to do so, because they are wealthier and more stable economies are a result of a history of exploitation of others; or even, sometimes, they are directly responsible for creating the state of state collapse that created a particular group of refugees. This naturally creates feelings of resentment, and even compassion fatigue.

Perhaps the deeper fear is simply this: that in the body of the refugee we come to terms with the fragility of nationhood and stability. With the realization that when we are looking into the face of refugees, we are looking directly into our own possibility. That there is nothing but a weird grace, a ruthless machinery of state, and our own collusion with it, keeping us from becoming refugees ourselves. This realization, that identity is fluid and never actualized or ever stable, and our own denial of this, is at the heart of the human condition. We fear, and sometimes hate, refugees, because their existence is our deepest fear: that we don't and never will belong anywhere.

Contrary to all protestations, America is not really a nation of immigrants but rather of refugees. Trauma, displacement, and a fanatical hope have marked all Americans from the occupants of the Mayflower through every subsequent group who arrived, or were forcibly brought here. This is the unspoken and sometimes unacknowledged fear and fact of being American. This means that these unkind ghosts of our pasts, these specters of self and previous nations that will not be dismissed so easily always attend our daily negotiations around identity.

This is a complex negotiation because while we all feel the inexplicable tug of nostalgia to identify with all parts of our historical pasts, we are torn when we actually have to inhabit any of those pasts. The very word, nostalgia, in its original meaning refers to the pain from an old wound. The sentimentality that often accompanies nostalgia is just a way to bear the pain while we revisit the wound.

This is why the refugee is the most challenging and most romantic body to the modern sensibility because it carries all the marks of the shadow that we have buried or at least blunted, and simultaneously all the possibility of our current status. We realize when we confront the refugee that we are staring into the mirror of our own memories of displacement. We remember the pain of their loss, one that still resides deep within us, and it calls to our own suffering and then we are caught in a web of extreme difficulty: how to balance our compassion with the need to define the limits of hospitality—both of which are needed if we are to help our displaced friends find their dignity again.

All the anger, confusion, and irrational fear experienced by refugees or those working on behalf of these communities stems from these anxieties that the larger culture feels. It is not new, it is not uniquely American, but what is uniquely American is the shame and silence around these feelings. If we are to make any progress in this area, we must learn to talk, and to talk outside of the matrix of right and wrong, but rather learn to negotiate our fears and insecurities.

. . .

Eight-year-old Mark, walking in a long line of refugees and carrying me, is an image that stays with me. It haunts our relationship. The fact of my physical weight as an eight-month-old has merged with the weight of the trauma of the war that displaced us, becoming, for him, something he cannot put down for fear perhaps that it will die, and with it, something important about him. Because to be eight and have to carry a younger sibling for miles, on foot, afraid as you get tired that you might drop him, afraid of bullets, afraid of death, something that while real it still, undefinable in your eight-year-old mind, is unimaginable.

And war, regardless of what the distance of news or television might suggest, happens suddenly and even casually for most people it affects. It doesn't matter how many states of emergency are declared, how many curfews are imposed, what the local news tells you. Humans have a near infinite capacity to normalize the world in order to survive and to thrive.

In the months leading up to the secession of Biafra, hundreds of thousands of Igbos living in northern Nigeria were slaughtered in ethnic cleansing, their bodies despoiled and sent back to the eastern homelands of the Ibo as mutilated corpses packed into train carriages. Still, Igbo leaders tried to broker peace, tried to hold onto the hope of this new country called Nigeria. And so, although my father moved our family from the Igbo city of Igboagu where we lived, where my father, a former member of Parliament, was now school principal, back to ancestral town of Afikpo, the idea was we would be safe and could wait out the "troubles" in relative safety. And then one afternoon, while your mother is making lunch, a relative arrives to tell you that you have half an hour to gather your life together and flee. It takes most of us longer to pack for a day at work.

I often think of how hard this was for my mother, a white woman in a Nigerian war. To take four children, while pregnant with another, and to flee in a long line of refugees on foot. To face the possibility of violent death every day in the midst of the reality of hunger and loss and fear. To try to flee one country to another. To cross several hundred miles, a distance that in peacetime would be a four-hour drive, but now in this reality of war and death, takes two years, because the road is never straight. To attempt this journey to the only operational airstrip, a former road. To give birth to your only daughter in a hospital being strafed by enemy bombs. To have left all but your youngest boy in the trust of other refugees to flee ahead of the bombs trusting you will find each other again. To keep the youngest boy, barely a year old with you, in that hospital with bombs coming down while you're trying to give birth. To be attended only by a frightened nurse and a calm Irish nun-midwife who laid your son in the cot next to her cookies and Earl Grey tea. She would wheel both from ward to ward ahead of the bombs, the nurse doing the same to the mother. To bounce from country to country until your own home lets you in grudgingly. All of these experiences never leave you.

A friend of mine, also a former refugee, told me that the feeling is a bit like moving through the foster system, you always feel displaced, always feel like a burden, always feel outside of everything. I, like every refugee, have hundreds of stories of difficulty and danger and the potential loss of life and the perpetual journey to healing.

There are many things that trigger these bittersweet memories. For me the smell of Earl Grey tea is a strong one, comfort and struggle, the knowledge that I'm always traveling away from refugee. If the road is kind, one day I will arrive.

Last, First, Middle

JOSEPH AZAM

M ost days I hide in plain sight. I am a Muslim refugee from a war-torn country—the sum of many fears—camouflaged by the trappings of Anglo-American-ness: fair skin, a mastery of the American vernacular, a picture of my blue-eyed wife and daughter on my desk at work, and called by a name that my late grandfather would not recognize.

I am an Afghan-American. My parents, Ashraf and Nina, like many Afghans in the late 1970s and early 1980s, fled from Afghanistan as the country became a frontline in the Cold War. In 1980, they made it as far as Virginia, where some of their friends, also émigrés from Afghanistan, had settled. They set about to build a life there, but they were interrupted when my grandfather Haji Mohammad Azam—my father's father—fell ill back in Kabul with a failing heart. In 1981, not knowing the extent of my grandfather's illness, my parents returned to Afghanistan to be at his side. My mother was four months pregnant with me at the time.

Choosing to go back into a war zone with no guarantee of a second escape spoke volumes about how precious my grandfather was in our family and my parents' dedication to him. That, combined with the strong pull of their ancestral soil, made a decision that many would have considered difficult an easy one for them.

One of the deep pains in my life is that I never got to know my grandfather, my *baba jaan*; I have only a handful of photos and not a single memory of him. He knew me though. Throughout my childhood my parents would frequently remind me of his strong attachment to me. Family lore is that my mother's pregnancy is what kept him alive. His longing to meet me, they say, willed his deteriorating body to carry on through the late stages of heart failure. After I was born, his love for me and my parents' sense of our fleeting time together in Kabul led them to ask him to choose my name.

My baba jaan was a man of deep faith so having received this task from my parents that was the first place he turned. The story, as it's been recounted to me over the years, is that he sat down with his well-worn Quran and asked God to guide his hands as he opened it to a random page, a page that turned out to be the beginning of the *Surah Yousuf*, the narrative of the prophet Yousuf. Known for its lessons in righteousness, courage, patience, and forgiveness, the twelfth *surah* of the Quran is regarded by Muslims as one of its most beautiful and lucid. For my grandfather, this was a revelation.

He named me Mohammad Yousuf Azam. These names—his first and most generous gifts to me—were weighty, meaningful, and, I've always assumed, a mark of his aspirations for me. The name Mohammad I shared with my two grandfathers and my father, who, like millions of other Muslims, carried it in the hope of being able to follow a path as virtuous as Prophet Mohammad. My name was a product of my grandfather's hopes and conviction; it was my inheritance.

In the months after I was born, Afghanistan fell deeper into turmoil. These were the early days of the Soviet occupation, a period marked by raids on civilians and the razing of entire towns considered by the Soviet-backed forces to be strongholds of the, at times, equally brutal Afghan resistance movement. Kabul, where my family was from, was the epicenter of the chaos.

Both sides of my family had always been politically active in Afghanistan in one form or another. They were writers and industrialists with a strong love of country and an equally fierce penchant for outspokenness. My mother was the daughter of a political prisoner. Her father, Mohammad Tahir Besmil, along with a number of her uncles, spent over a decade in prison for their part in trying to orchestrate a takeover of the Afghan monarchy long before the Russians ever set their sights on the country. For my family, the rumors of house-to-house raids and hasty arrests rang too familiar. With Kabul becoming more dangerous by the day and with the blessing of their families, my parents decided to leave again, this time likely for good. The question then became how.

At the time, in addition to aggressively seeking out dissidents, the Russian-aligned government in Kabul was systematically conscripting men of fighting age, going door-to-door as if demanding alms for the poor.

Families, mine included, would routinely send away or hide their young men knowing that, once taken, the likelihood of their return from the brutal war was slim. My parents worried that trying to leave the country with my father, thirty years old at the time, would bring him exactly the sort of attention they desperately wanted to avoid. So they chose to split up and leave the country separately. Their plan was to make their way back to America but, as is the case for many refugees today, the path there was neither direct nor without peril.

My parents settled on Berlin as an eventual rendezvous point. My father had studied in Germany as a young man and his family had business contacts there that they thought would be useful in securing a visa to leave Kabul discreetly. Because she had no idea how long it would take him to be able to secure this visa, my mother resigned herself to being alone with me for some indeterminate length of time.

The thought of his young daughter-in-law languishing indefinitely on her own in a foreign land with his newest grandchild was unbearable for my baba jaan, who intervened to see if there was a way he could be with us until my father made his safe exit. Given the difficulty he knew he would have in obtaining a German visa, he suggested that my mother and I leave Afghanistan through neighboring India, then he could join us there while we waited for my father to find his way out. My mother, just twenty years old at the time, about to be a refugee for a second time and carrying a four-month-old baby, was glad to have the company, so she agreed. In a matter of weeks we were off to Delhi. My grandfather, in one of his final acts of devotion and in spite of his failing health, followed closely behind us.

India was safe if not pleasant, but then again our notion of safety was relative back then. Years after our time there my mother recounted stories of the unnerving poverty and desperation she encountered, as well as the many unexpected indignities she, like so many refugees, experienced on her journey to safety. One particularly harrowing incident involved an overnight ride on a dangerously overcrowded train during which we ended up in a bottom bunk only to realize that there was an incontinent elderly man in the bunk above. Too shocked to disturb him, too afraid to complain, and too cramped to move, all she could do to keep me calm and distract herself from the dripping urine-soaked mattress above her was to breastfeed me through the night. As she quickly discovered, India was no place for a young refugee mother, at least not mine, to be. So, with the prospect of my father's visa to Germany still uncertain, my mother made a decision to head to Berlin early, leaving India and my grandfather behind.

Several months went by before my father managed to leave Afghanistan. When he finally arrived in Berlin we wasted little time before making our way to New York City to seek asylum and start our life together as a family. My baba jaan never did end up making it back to Kabul. Not long after he got word in India that we made it to Berlin, he left this world to find his own peace.

. . .

Living in New York brought with it two things families like mine were eager to have: opportunity and anonymity. My mother, who had studied early education in Afghanistan and had been a schoolteacher in Kabul, started working almost as soon as she landed. The only English she knew she had picked up waiting tables at a pizza shop in Virginia during her first stint in the United States. so she sought out work that demanded she say very little. Her first job in New York was sweeping floors and providing treatments at a beauty spa on the Upper East Side of Manhattan. My father, who had studied economics and was fluent in German and French, started off selling newspapers at a corner kiosk in midtown Manhattan, not far from Rockefeller Center—where my office is today. The three of us lived in a one-bedroom apartment in Flushing, Queens, while my parents saved money to start a business selling imported Middle Eastern rugs and tapestries.

While they eventually opened a rug gallery in the shadow of the Empire State building, their business began from the back of an old Chevy van that my father crisscrossed the United States in, with me riding shotgun on occasion. From time to time, an African American Muslim man named Hossein, whom my father had hired to help with the long drives, joined us. Of all the trips I took in that van, I remember the trips with Hossein most vividly.

Our van only had two seats so when Hossein was with us I would get to lie across the stack of dusty rugs in the back, intoxicated by the distinctive perfume of mothballs as my mind wandered. I remember watching our headlights cut through the otherwise unbroken darkness on overnight sprints, amazed at how boundless America seemed. On those drives and in those early years it felt like all of it was mine and I didn't have anyone around me to make me feel otherwise.

My father's family business in Afghanistan had been in shoes and leather. His family had owned several factories and shops in Kabul so it made sense that our New York rug business eventually evolved into a men's shoe store, where I started working before I was old enough to read. I can't recall the addresses of many of the places we lived when I was growing up but the address of that store, 264 Fifth Avenue, is etched in my mind; it was the only place I could see my parents most weeks. It was home, and the revolving cast of characters my parents hired to work there—almost exclusively African and Caribbean immigrants—became family.

New York in the 1980s, at least the part that I grew up in, was full of families like mine who had recently come from some distant place in search of a better life. I went to school with a lot of kids from those families and it wasn't hard to spot us if you knew what to look for. We were the ones who dressed a little differently and carried our lunches in repurposed plastic shopping bags that could never be tied tightly enough to contain the unfamiliar aromas from our home kitchens. You would have found us tagging along with our parents for parent-teacher meetings to help translate and working at our family-run businesses on the weekends. We stood out and were each vulnerable in our own way.

While I grew up not necessarily knowing what a refugee was or that I was one, I don't recall ever not knowing the feeling of being an outsider. It didn't help that for years the only identification I had was a green card with the words Resident Alien across the top. As a child I watched helplessly as my parents struggled, like many refugees do, to integrate into the United States. I became fixated on the notion of being somehow displaced myself. Even my name itself, like my green card, became a billboard for my foreignness.

Growing up, my name—Mohammad—caused me to dread the fall. While some kids fretted about months of monotony, my angst was focused squarely on the first moments of the school year when roll would be taken out loud for the first time. By the first grade, I had come up with a routine designed to ensure that my teacher wouldn't even utter the name Mohammad. Before the start of the first day of class, while most kids were saying goodbye to their parents or getting reacquainted with friends, I would seek out my new teacher to ask that they call me by my "real first name," Yousuf. The modest bargain I made with myself was that I would live with Yousuf, which sounded enough like Joseph to get me by, but I would rid myself of the name Mohammad, which I could not fashion into anything that could pass. And for whatever it's worth, I wasn't alone in making these sorts of compromises.

I had a lot of friends from immigrant families with strange sounding names and most of them went even further than I did in trying to fortify their American-ness. Instead of going by their given names, many of them took on noms de guerre like Michael, or Danny, or Jessica in the struggle to fit in. I never had the courage or the permission to go that far myself. I had abandoned Mohammad, but I never asked to be called Joseph or Joe, in part because it felt dishonest but mostly because I was worried about my parents somehow finding out and seeing it as a rejection of who we were. Ironically enough, years later they would do it for me.

. . .

In 1996, worn down by New York, my parents moved us to Orange County, California, a place that glimmered with blinding affluence and whiteness. One of the first places I went when we landed in California was my soon-to-be high school in Dana Point. I was a sophomore at the time, and while I never expressed to my parents the unease I felt in moving there, they recognized it. The effort I had put into curating my identity in New York, the ways I had come up with for managing my otherness—all of it would need to start anew, or so I thought.

When it came time to enroll me in school, my father made a choice that short-circuited my unrest, at least for a time. As we stood there at the registrar's counter, he very casually, and without so much as turning to me, registered me as Joseph Azam. To this day I don't know what went into his decision. Perhaps he and my mother had noticed my mushrooming anxiety, and, perhaps they realized it had something to do with how I thought I was going to fare in this new place. In any case, my father's decision liberated me from the immigrant self-gaze that had consumed me for so long, but it also felt like a death.

So much of what I had been through with my parents over the years—Kabul, India, Germany, our early days in New York—seemed to fall instantly out of focus as the name Yousuf faded. Being known as Joseph or Joe outside of my family brought with it the ordinariness and anonymity that I had so desperately wanted at age six, but at fifteen it brought me discomfort and waves of guilt at home.

I wondered what went through my parents' heads when they'd call me down for dinner by a new name or if my young sisters, who quickly took to calling me Joe, would eventually forget the name they had called me when they first learned to speak. I wondered whether it stung my parents that on top of the many things they lost and left behind in Kabul, a decade and a half later they felt compelled to surrender my name as well. More than anything, I brooded over what my grandfather would have thought of the way in which I had treated his exquisite gift to me.

I'll never know exactly how or to what extent going through high school under an alias colored my experience, or whether or not it somehow helped clear a path for me—to college back in New York, to graduate school, to law school, to a career in corporate America. What it did do was leave me with an entirely new dilemma over what was worse: being identifiably foreign or secretly false. It was a question I tortured myself with throughout high school and one that was thrown into relief not long after I graduated at a U.S. Citizenship and Immigration Services Center just south of Los Angeles.

My parents had become naturalized U.S. citizens when I was very young but hadn't gotten around to filling out the paperwork for me to claim my derivative citizenship until we had moved to California. I was eighteen years old by the time my application was up for review, which meant I had to go in for a citizenship interview as part of the process. I remember breezing through my interview and sitting in a drab corridor in the immigration center as I waited to submit my passport application that same day. The fluorescent lights above my head had lulled me into a trance when my eyes suddenly fixated on the first fields of the still blank application: Name (Last, First, Middle); Place of Birth; Address; List All Other Names You Have Used.

No sooner had I realized the choice that lay in front of me than my number was called; I found myself standing with my father at a counter once again being asked to register my name. This time the decision was mine alone to make, he made sure of that. At a loss for what to do and with an impatient clerk scowling at my empty form I panicked and dropped the stack of documents that I had been toting around all morning. Realizing that she had frazzled me, even if she was unsure of why, the clerk behind the counter told me to take my time gathering myself and cleaning up my mess. She had no idea how many years I had spent trying to do just that.

As I knelt down to pull together the papers that had fallen around my feet, I was confronted by the dissonance that I had lived with for so many years. I picked up the green card with the photo of Yousuf, the wide-eyed asylum seeker. I picked up the California driver's license with the awkward photo of Joseph, the gangly teenager who had just barely passed his driving test. I picked up my parents' citizenship certificates. I picked up duplicate after duplicate I had brought of my various citizenship forms that outlined in detail the places we had lived. I picked up my passport application and I picked up my pen.

What I did next is simply what felt most honest. Instead of choosing between my names, I chose all of them.

Joseph Mohammad Yousuf Azam. It was disjointed, redundant perhaps, but it made whole again the hopes of my grandfather and added to them my own. It didn't fit in the space provided on the form that day but it fit the moment and it fit me.

This was my American name.

Common Story

DAVID BEZMOZGIS

On September 8, 1979, my parents and I boarded a train at Riga station and left the Soviet Union. I was six. My mother was thirty-two. My father was about to turn forty-four, the age I am now. My parents had sold our possessions and paid the Soviet authorities an exorbitant fee to renounce our citizenships, rendering us stateless. Accompanying us to the station were a small number of friends and relatives—those unafraid to be seen with traitors to the motherland. When they said goodbye it was not with the routine *do svidaniya* (until we meet again), but the melancholy *proshchay* (farewell forever).

I think about what it must have been like for my parents at this moment. In the bustle of loading the belongings and exchanging last words, they must have felt the shock of finality, of realizing that what was happening could not be rescinded or revised. The possessions had been sold, the apartment vacated, the jobs abandoned. Wherever they ended up, they wouldn't know the language, and my father, whose career had been in athletics, would almost certainly have to find other work. The life they knew was over and they had only a dim sense of what the future held. What's more, they hadn't necessarily needed to go. They weren't fleeing war or genocide, but only the economic shambles of the Soviet Union and its habitual, endemic anti-Semitism. But this wasn't new. They'd lived with it all their lives. Neither idealists nor iconoclasts, they were taking a gamble simply because an opportunity had presented itself and others had seized it.

Visas for Israel, our "ancestral homeland," had enabled us to leave the Soviet Union, but when we arrived in Vienna my parents declared their desire to go to some other Western country. We applied to the United Nations High Commissioner for Refugees and were registered as refugees. We stayed for two weeks in Vienna and four months on the outskirts of Rome while our case was processed. In Australia, my father had a distant aunt whom he'd never met, but to whom my parents had shipped a collection of the Russian classics, which they'd acquired with great difficulty and at considerable expense. My father's younger sister had emigrated a few years earlier and landed in Los Angeles, but we received a letter from her husband dissuading us from even thinking about joining them. *Take a cold shower*, he wrote. Friends from Riga applied to Atlanta and my parents prepared to follow suit. But in the end, we wound up in Toronto, where we didn't know anyone. I still consider it strange how random this all was, and sometimes wonder about the lives we would have had, the different person I would have become, in Melbourne or Los Angeles, Atlanta or Israel—or Riga, had we stayed there as others did.

For many of the people who emigrated with us, it wasn't their first experience of exile. Most Soviet Jews of my parents' or grandparents' generation survived World War II because they managed to flee Hitler's army. Those who remained behind met almost certain death. In the summer of 1941, when my father was almost six years old, about the same age I was when we left Riga, he, along with his parents and two sisters, boarded one of the last trains out of Daugavpils. At one point along the journey, they were attacked by a German plane and a piece of shrapnel sliced his father's boot but, miraculously, not his foot. For four years, his family lived deep inside Russia, a time characterized by constant hunger. It stayed with him for the rest of his life. If food was ever left out, he ate it. I sometimes came into the kitchen to find him eating butter.

Not until writing this essay did it occur to me to wonder if my father knew Russian when his family fled there. He had been born in independent Latvia to a Jewish family and arguably wouldn't have needed to speak anything but Yiddish and Latvian. Of course, even if he didn't know Russian, he probably picked it up fast. From experience, I know how much easier it is for a child to learn a language than an adult. My maternal grandfather, also a Latvian Jew, spoke Russian imperfectly when he fled the Nazis. Near Pskov, he wanted to volunteer for the Red Army and asked a local Russian boy to direct him to the recruiting station. Because of his poor Russian, the boy took him instead to the office of the NKVD, and reported him as a German spy. Only a fortunate coincidence kept him from being shot.

In fiction and in essays, I've written about different aspects of our emigration and my family's history, but I feel I have only a partial understanding of it and always will. Every now and then, I learn something new. Recently, my mother and I recalled the accident I had shortly after we settled in Toronto. I fell from the jungle gym at the school playground and broke my elbow. I was with my cousin, a year younger than me. I'd always understood we were by ourselves because our parents were attending English classes. My mother corrected me. She and my father weren't at the classes but at a hospital to see a gynecologist for a problem she'd been having and she thought that her sister and brother-in-law were watching us. The damage to my elbow was extensive and required surgery. I didn't speak English and couldn't understand what the doctors and nurses were saying. My father was obliged to attend the English classes or else lose the government support that covered our rent and food. So my mother sat by my bedside for days, comforting me, worrying about me, understanding little more than I did of what the doctors and nurses were saying, and, secretly, bleeding. She thought she would go crazy.

Soon thereafter, she suffered a nervous breakdown. For days, she couldn't get out of bed. I remember paramedics coming to our apartment, putting her on a gurney, and taking her away. At this time, my grandmother came to visit us from Israel. My mother's parents and her younger brother left Riga when we did, but elected to go to Israel, largely because my grandfather—the one who was almost shot by the NKVD—was a lifelong Zionist. I don't remember my grandmother's visit and I didn't know that she'd earned the money for the plane ticket by cleaning hotel rooms. She'd planned the trip because she missed her daughters and grandchildren, not because she knew my mother was falling apart. But she came to our apartment and was shocked to see what had become of my mother. She cooked and cleaned and put us back on our feet.

I don't relate these things to ennoble my parents and relatives. They weren't heroes in the Soviet Union and the experience of immigration didn't turn them into ones. Once they established themselves, they didn't particularly sympathize with other refugees. Rather, their attitude toward them was skeptical—if not cynical. Their politics are conservative; in America, most of them would have voted for Trump. When I challenge them on this, they dismiss me as naïve. They see no incongruity. Those other refugees—particularly brown and Muslim—are not like them.

Actually, in the only way that matters, those other refugees *are* like them. They are not paragons of virtue, but flawed and unexceptional people who adhere to the basic tenets of the social contract. Because, fundamentally, what do modern democracies ask of their citizens? To obey the laws and pay their taxes. If they have done nothing else, my family has done that.

Well, modern democracies ask a little more, but often accept the rudiments of abiding by the laws and paying taxes. At a Canadian citizenship ceremony for my American wife, the officiant encouraged the new Canadians to embrace the civic values of their adoptive land and discard old enmities and hatreds. He emphasized the importance of exercising their franchise and of volunteering their time. An earnest and awkward representative of the local Rotary Club talked up the merits of his organization and provided free juice and cookies. There were one hundred new Canadians at the ceremony. I watched them go up and accept their certificates. Among these were families with small children, dressed up for the occasion, as my parents and I had been three decades earlier. But the origins of these new immigrants had changed. Most appeared to be from the Middle East and South Asia, many with Muslim names. Driving home, I remarked to my wife that white supremacists would not have liked the look of that room.

"Good," she said.

"Neither good or bad," I said.

It was just a fact, value neutral.

What is a country? Who is a citizen? Where do we belong? What do we owe one another? Why have we organized ourselves the way we have? The questions sound trite but I found myself dwelling on them recently at an Immigration and Refugee Board of Canada hearing. At the request of a writers' organization, I agreed to serve as an observer in solidarity with a writer I'd never met. For three hours, I sat in the hearing room with another representative of the writers' organization, the writer, his lawyer, an interpreter, and the adjudicator (who interrogated the writer's harsh and tumultuous life), testing, not unfairly, apparent inconsistencies and lapses in his story. For instance, if a man receives a terrifying phone call in which his life is threatened, does he remain in his parents' house for several weeks while he awaits his travel documents? If he fears the police because they are complicit with the religious fanatics who hate his books, and if these same police abuse him in a vile and despicable way, could he not evade them by moving to another city inside his own country?

They were reasonable questions. The writer countered them with the peculiar logic and idiosyncrasy of a human life—much of which could not be substantiated. But he came from a place where the things he described were plausible and they were worse than anything my parents experienced in the Soviet Union. He'd had the bad luck to be born at the wrong time between the wrong borders. His government was as glad to be rid of him as he was to have left. He believed he was better suited to Canada. From what I could see, he was right. Even if it was discovered that he was being less than fully truthful, I thought he was harmless. But it was as likely as not that he would be sent back. The case could be made that he had arrived under false pretenses while others sat in their miserable countries or in displaced persons camps waiting to be admitted. Was it fair that he should be allowed to stay? Then again, he was already here and the country was big and could accommodate thousands like him without anyone noticing. And yet so much effort had been invested into deciding his claim. Months of preparation. Documents filed. A room reserved. All of us assembled. The proceedings conducted with utmost gravity. Politicians defining themselves by it. Families quarreling and becoming estranged. But the longer I sat in the room, the more arbitrary it seemed.

At the end of the three hours, the adjudicator still hadn't rendered his verdict. His interrogation had run long. The lawyer hadn't had a chance to question his client. It was resolved that we would return in a month. The outstanding issues remained: credibility, identity, delay, objective risk, and subjective fear.

Flesh and Sand

FATIMA BHUTTO

I

I am not in a dream. I am wide awake.

I am standing at the entrance of the Fondazione Prada in Milan, holding a piece of paper in my hand. I have checked away my bag and my phone and my pens; the paper is the only thing I have with me. With my signature, I have promised that I am of sound mind and body, am aware some of the images I will see may be disturbing, and am prepared to assume all risks. No one under the age of sixteen is allowed to experience Alejandro G. Inarritu's Carne y Arena, a virtual reality installation and exhibition. I sign the waiver, making promises with the first letters and last letters of my name.

Inarritu designed the simulation to be experienced alone. Each visitor must enter and travel through the director's landscape of Mexican-American border, by themselves, helpless and undefended. From beginning to end, it will be a twenty-minute experience. I hold the paper with my signature and my promises folded in my hands and wait in the October sunshine for my turn. I'm not afraid.

II

Virtual reality is built somewhere between the borders of the real and the imaginary, between the truth and a lie. Using 3D imagery, you can now sit in your home and be transported across the boundaries of time, distance, and space. Standing in your living room, you can walk across the ivory white marble floors of the Taj Mahal, or skydive off a cliff, or fight alongside weary soldiers in a guerilla war. At the rate that technology is radically progressing, it will force us to question what is real and what is a dream more and more. Optimists like Chris Milk, who runs a VR studio called Here Be Dragons, say this technology will be the "ultimate empathy machine," connecting people to each other in the most profound way. The worriers wonder how we will regulate it, how we will protect ourselves, and what social conventions we can uphold in a world of the unreal. When people think they are dreaming, they do crazy things— violence, life, love, so many things become easy and cheap.

Facebook, Google, Samsung, and Sony have all created their own virtual reality headsets. With the right cameras and software, today anyone can create multidimensional content. Oculus Rift, the technology used in Carne y Arena, was born to enhance the world of video gaming. But VR has traveled beyond the world of teenage boys. It has the potential to change the way we watch movies, how we travel, the way we fight wars, the way we explore, hurt, and heal.

Cedars-Sinai hospital in Los Angeles is already using VR as a "pharmacy," Sophie Hackford, a London-based futurist, says, transporting patients to relaxing and soothing environments before traumatic surgery. With a headset and a pair of headphones, burn victims in excruciating pain are clicked into cold locations and just the imagination, the virtual imagery of snow and ice, has been found to release them from the physical confines of their pain 60 percent more efficiently than morphine. The world of VR is now so sophisticated that it has the power to trick our brain into believing that what we watch through our headsets is real—even though we know, intellectually and emotionally—that we are just spectators in a beautiful, elaborate show.

III

I enter through a dark room and am told to read Inarritu's welcome message and follow the instructions through a dark warehouse. There is no exhibition map, no clue as to when the real will fade away to the virtual. I don't remember if it is quiet or if there is music because I am aware, suddenly, that I'm alone. I walk toward a door and open it. Along the walls are steel benches. The room is white, lit by bright halogen lamps. Everywhere along the floor—under the benches, in the corner, gathered in small piles—are shoes. There are men's sandals, dust marking the soft pads where toes once pressed against the leather, large moccasins without any soles, women's broken high heels, a baby's rubbery tennis shoe.

1. Take off your socks and shoes. 2. Put them in the locker. 3. Sit down and wait for the alarm, when it rings go through the door. The instructions are written in red on the walls.

I hesitate but don't follow the instructions. I walk beside the steel benches and bend down to look at the shoes. It takes me a moment to notice the silence and when I do, it is piercing, like a dog whistle, and terrifying. But just as I get used to it, above me, below me, around me, there is a thunderous noise, like a train rushing over my head, and the entire room feels as though it shakes.

They call this room *la hielera*, the icebox. If you are caught migrating across the desert between Mexico and America, border patrol puts you in a freezing cold concrete holding cell. According to a 2015 Freedom of Information Act request by the American Immigration Council, most migrants are kept in these notorious cells for two days on average.

On the wall, between the instructions I'm still ignoring as I wait for the alarm to ring—*it doesn't ring, why doesn't it?*—a script in red tells me that these are the shoes left behind by those who died trying to cross the border into the United States. Six thousand people died over a seven-year period. The noise comes again. My whole body tenses as I wait for it to pass. Maybe I have to take off my shoes, maybe the alarm won't ring until I do—*why hasn't it rung?*—and for the passing of a few seconds, as long as the sound of the screaming train, I think: I want to leave.

I take off my shoes and put them in the locker. I have no idea how long I have been in the icebox but now I'm cold. They will tell me afterward it's only about two minutes. I sit on the steel bench and pull my legs up to rest my bare feet on the edge, hugging my knees to my chest, like I did when I was at school and didn't want to play. There is no clock. I have no phone. I'm still holding my waiver, folded up in the palm of my hand. I watch the alarm. It doesn't ring.

IV

I was born in Kabul, Afghanistan. My mother is Afghan but my father was Pakistani. My displacement was my father's and though it was comfortable, though there were dining tables of food and books borrowed from libraries and school, it was—like all displacements—born out of a history of violence and sorrow.

Three years before I was born, my grandfather, my father's father, Zulfikar Ali Bhutto, Pakistan's first democratically elected head of state, had been overthrown by a military coup and killed. Three years after I was born, my father's younger brother was murdered. My father, Mir Murtaza, was a political exile and he moved from his home country of Pakistan to Kabul, and then after my birth, as war erupted across Afghanistan, we traveled to Damascus, Syria. What peace we managed to build as a family always blossomed in the shadow of that violence and our years were spent with the knowledge that its pursuit was never far behind us, no matter what borders and what distance we had crossed. For all our happiness together, we knew that it could end, like the lives we had already left behind, brutally and without warning.

I was fourteen when my father was killed outside our home. He was a member of parliament and a critic of the government's corruption and violence. More than one hundred policemen lined the roads along our house that night; they shut the streetlights and waited on the dark pavements, some of them in sniper positions in the nearby banyan trees, for my father to come home. He was shot several times and left to bleed on the street. We could hear everything inside, we were just footsteps away, but were blocked from exiting our gate by the police.

My father had only just returned to his country after nearly two decades in exile. It was supposed to be a happy homecoming but what met us in our own country, after years of being strangers in other lands, was grief. As a child and a young woman I was told one copes with this constant, unceasing sense of dislocation and violence by being brave. But now, my safety from all this dangerous knowledge comes partly from another source—knowing that none of it is real.

The difference between Eastern and Western cultures is *maya*: illusion.

In the East, we believe that all life is maya. Inherently, we are suspicious of time, we don't believe in space or distance, and our sense of all things bends to the knowledge of this fact— nothing is real. Not life, not rules, not order, nothing. Between the dream and the real, we have no boundaries, both are fused together. The lie and the truth are the same. Everything is an illusion created by the mind.

In the West, your life exists in clear, certain terms. This is good, that is bad. This is heaven, that is hell. This is true, that is false. Where we have dreams, you have total, pure reality.

In a future that promises to be shaped by virtual reality, who will be more comfortable in a dream?

V

Beneath me, there is cold gravel. Sand. I walk barefoot, treading softly on the cool, rough floor. "Your body never lies," Inarritu said in an interview after Carne y Arena launched at the 70th Festival de Cannes this spring. It's why we have to walk without shoes, flesh to sand, it's why we go alone into the dark chambers of this exhibition.

Two girls speak to me in English with a thick Italian accent. One places a bag on my back, the other lowers the Oculus headset over my eyes. Be curious, the girl with the goggles says, look around, but don't run.

Why would I run? I think, but don't ask.

They will be there, the girl says, to make sure I don't run

(*why would I run!*) and to pull me back by the bag if I get too close to the walls. Be curious, walk around, she repeats. Someone puts a pair of headphones on me and as I blink, the light around me transforms from darkness to the cold blue light of the desert, delicate like the colors of a kerosene lamp. I turn slowly, my feet crunching against the gravel—I can hear it—and though behind me the sky is still dark and broken, the color of ink, I can make out the shadow of Joshua trees.

And then, I hear people.

There's a man, the coyote, and he's on the phone, he's walking toward me and I freeze. Is he talking to me?

One man becomes two then three then more and the light opens across the horizon and the people are closer, so close that I can see a woman, middle-aged and heavyset. She can't breathe properly and she needs help walking. I move to help her—my brain knows but doesn't know that this is an illusion—maya—but before I do, I feel a chill and I step aside, careful so she doesn't walk into me. I don't touch her. If I had, I would have seen her heart—red and throbbing—beat through her body. Any contact with the migrants in this VR landscape sets off their beating hearts, a reminder to us spectators that somewhere, these people are real. I find that out afterward, just as I find out that none of these people, these illusions, are actors. They are real. Inarritu interviewed migrants from Guatemala, El Salvador, and Mexico and asked them to collaborate on this installation. Together, they reenacted real journeys, reliving real danger, even wearing the same clothes they had on when they walked across the desert to enter Arizona.

I walk in small steps (partially because what are those two girls doing if not watching me? I am being watched just like I am watching others, a dream within a dream within a dream. I am not afraid). There are white flowers in the desert bushes, like camellias, and I almost bend to pick one. A blue plastic bag floats in the distance and for a second I hope it's not me that dropped it. Birds glide through the sky and people walk all around me, slowly, wearily, their feet dragging.

And then there is the beating sensation of a helicopter in the sky and my body moves instinctively to find safety from it. When I look at my feet I can see the earth rustling, blown into the air by the movement of the helicopter's blades. I can feel the pulsing of those blades in my eardrums. I can see the face of the middle-aged woman, down to the furrows of her brow. Her name is Lina, I find out later; she is fifty-three years old and crossed this border after a long journey from Guatemala, and the fear etched in her face is a mirror of my own.

I can hear a child cry, he's next to me, near me, as two jeeps of border patrol guards come out of nowhere. There is a German Shepherd barking, spitting, and a man pointing a semi-automatic in my face.

I have had guns pointed at me before; in real life. I have been in a landscape, far from this, with dust and dirt and young men shouting with weapons raised and the threat of violence flowing between us and at this moment, I cannot separate those memories from this. Just as I can hear a child cry, I can feel my heart beat, I can hear it drumming against my body, and every-thing that I know:

that it's October,
I'm in Milan—at Prada!
I hold the two folded pages of a waiver in my hand,

I am in a summer dress because this morning the sun was
    gentle but persistent,
my shoes are in a locker,
that I can step out of the gun sight and run, even though I
    promised not to, right into the wall
that one of the two Italian girls will most likely protect me
    from running straight into the wall,
                   (hopefully)
that this very installation/experience/narrative that I'm
    in is only 6.5 minutes long, that people have gone in
    before me and will go in after me, that it will be over
    in January
that I don't live here, I can leave here and go anywhere—
    to any place in the world—all of that fades away and
    I can only feel my heart racing, beating behind the
    walls of my breast.

Perspective and What Gets Lost

THI BUI

How Succulent Food Defeated
Trump's Wall Before It Has Been Built

ARIEL DORFMAN

The wall, the wall. From the start, Donald Trump's campaign that would lead him to conquer the White House was fueled by the nativist card he played, the threat to the United States posed, according to his tirades, by the "aliens" who have swarmed across the border from Mexico, described as a bunch of "bad hombres," rapists, criminals, and drug dealers. Though, of course, he made a point of attesting to his love for Hispanics by tweeting a photo of himself eating a taco bowl in Trump Tower Grill in order to celebrate Cinco de Mayo in 2016. Given his tenuous grasp of his own country's history, there can be no doubt that he did not know then or now that the date commemorates the defeat by Mexico of a foreign enemy, France, back in 1862. A pity, because he would do well to ponder the traits with which the commander of the Mexican army characterized the head of the invading troops: arrogance, foolishness, and ineptitude—*soberbia, necedad, y torpeza*.

The very features Trump exhibited as he munched his taco bowl and dreamt of deporting (at least) eleven million "illegals" and build a huuuge and beautiful wall to keep them from ever coming back, a wall whose costs, he continues to promise, will be paid for by Mexico. A claim that he knows has no basis whatsoever in reality, so much so that when the president of Mexico, according to a leaked transcript of a phone call with him surfaced, insisted that his country would not pay for the wall, Trump demanded that such a position not be revealed to the press.

What Trump does not seem to realize is that this is a battle he has already lost. No, I am not talking about the unfeasibility of constructing parts of his wall in the middle of the immense Rio Grande, shared by both countries. Or how he would need to defile sacred Native American land. Or the requirement that the wall be transparent enough to see the other side and simultaneously made of materials dense enough to withstand erosion and therefore opaque. Or what an impossible engineering feat it would be to rise high enough to keep out drones and deep enough to discourage tunnels that, so far, have thwarted every effort to be blocked. Or that landowners in Texas are suing the government invoking their property rights and the Center for Biological Diversity, along with an Arizona congressman, is going to court to demand an environmental review of the irreparable damage to public lands and wildlife. Or that the $1.6 billion that Congressional Republicans wish to appropriate for the wall has no chance of passing the Senate, except if there is a government shutdown (which would also mean shutting down the blessed barrier itself). No, I am talking about a more modest foe of his proposal. Even before the first brick is laid, his wall has been vanquished by the very taco bowl he grins at demonically in his Twitter post, vanquished by that taco bowl and its many undocumented food cousins from all over Latin America.

What? Undocumented food as the unsung hero, ready to foil Trump's dream of an ethnically pure America?

As proof of what some readers may consider a startling assertion, I offer a store that my wife and I frequent here in

Durham, North Carolina, where we have settled after decades of wandering. I am sure that Trump's busy schedule (replete with gold outings and his meetings with authentically "bad hombres" like the dictator Sisi of Egypt or the murderous Duterte of the Philippines) does not contemplate coming to this town where Hillary Clinton received 78.9 percent of the votes in 2016, the highest victory in the whole state. But if the Donald, a former wrestler who claims to relish a good brawl, were indeed to venture into this adversarial territory, I would recommend that he stop by a supermarket that Angélica and I visit, at times for convenience's sake but more often to indulge in personal nostalgia.

I can savor under its vast roof the presence of the continent where I was born, go back, so to speak, to my own plural origins. On one shelf, Nobleza Gaucha, the yerba maté my Argentine parents used to sip every morning in their New York exile—my mother with sugar, my father in its more bitter version. Even to contemplate the bag that this grass herb comes in, allows me to recall how anxiously *mi mamá y mi papá* awaited shipments from the authoritarian Buenos Aires they had escaped in the forties. A bit further along in the store, I come upon *leche condensada en una lata*, the sort I would sip from a can on adolescent camping trips into the mountains of Chile, where my family moved when I was twelve. And nearby, a tin of Nido, the powdered milk my wife Angélica and I first fed our son Rodrigo as a baby, almost half a century ago in Santiago. Or Nesquik *para niños*, the chocolate we relied on to sweeten the existence of our younger son Joaquín, when he accompanied us back to Chile after many years of exile from Pinochet's dictatorship.

Origins, however, are never merely personal, but deeply collective, and especially so for Latin Americans such as myself, who feel an *entrañable* fellowship with natives from other unfortunate countries of our region. A stubborn history of thwarted dreams has led to a shared sense of purpose and sorrow, hope and resilience, which joins us all emotionally, beyond geographic destiny or national boundaries. To stroll up and down the grocery aisles of that store is to reconnect with the people and the lands and the tastebuds of those brothers and sisters and to partake, however vicariously, in meals being planned and prepared at that very moment in millions and millions of homes everywhere in the hemisphere. There is *canela* from Perú and *queso crema* from Costa Rica and *café torrado e moido* (*O sabor do campo na sua casa*) from Brazil. There is coconut juice from the Caribbean and frijoles of every possible and impossible variety and *maíz tostado* from Mexico and fresh *apio* (celery) from the Dominican Republic (they look like tiny twisted idols) and *hierbas medicinales para infusiones* from who knows where, and *albahaca* and *ajonjoli* and *linaza* and yuca and malanga and *chicharrones de cerdo* and *chicharrones de harina*.

If you were to go to São Paulo or Caracas or Quito, if you were to try to shop for this assortment of staples or delicacies in San José or La Paz or Bogotá, if you were to ask in any major or minor city of Latin America where you might be able to pick your way through such a plethora of culinary choices in one location, you would be told that a place like that does not exist anywhere in that country. There is no shop in Rio de Janeiro, for instance, that next to an array of carioca fare would allow you to select among eighteen multiplicities of chile peppers or buy Tampico punch or sample some *casabe* bread.

That is what is most fascinating about this grocery store sporting the name COMPARE—a name which cleverly works in Spanish and English and Portuguese—but the cleverness also reveals and revels in the fact that prices here are better than elsewhere, thus adhering to the same taco bowl philosophy of Donald Trump's capitalist aspirations, replete with commodities that can be exploited and competitors that need to be bested. But such self-evident commercialism, taking advantage of a niche in the market, does not detract from the astounding circumstance that in a small town of the Southern United States (population 267,587) there exists a greater representation of variegated Latin America than in Rio with its six and a half million inhabitants or in the megapolis of Ciudad de México with its twenty million.

This is what Donald Trump and his nativist cohorts need to understand: five hundred and twenty-five years after Cristobal Colón sighted the land that would be called by some other visionary's name, the sheer reality of a store like this one (and countless others like it all across the United States) resoundingly proves that the continent of Juárez and García Márquez and Eva Perón can no longer be understood to stop at the Rio Grande but extends far into the gringo North.

The food that hails me at that mega-Latino supermarket is not, of course, purely something that you sniff and peel, cook and devour. Hands reach for the potatoes that originated thousands of years ago in the Andean highlands, mouths water for the pineapple that the conquistadors did not know how to describe, bodies tremble at the thought of using their tongues, Proust-like, to return to a childhood home most of them will never see again. Behind hands and inside mouths and beyond bodies, there flourishes a cosmic piñata of stories, like mine, of escaping the native land, of alighting elsewhere, of crossing frontiers legally or surreptitiously, of border guards and guardian angels, of fighting to keep in touch with the vast *pueblo latinoamericano* left behind, of memories of hunger and repression and also of *solidaridad* and vivid dreams. A woman from Honduras is piling onto her cart a ton of bananas that are the color of a red sunset and, though well on their way to decomposing, will be perfect, she assures me, with tomatillos and pinto frijoles. A couple from Colombia (I detect the soft specificity of excellent Spanish from Bogotá) discuss whether to experiment and add to their *ajiaco* that night some Mexican serrano peppers (shining green as they curve under the neon light). The husband says that's fine, so long as she doesn't forget to mix in the *guascas* herb they have just bought and which he first relished when he was an infant. Inside each of them, as inside me and my Angélica, there is a tale of heart break and heart warmth, of hearths orphaned back home and hearths rekindled in our new dwellings.

Where else could these shoppers (and so many other unrecognized ambassadors from every country and ethnicity of the Americas) meet in such an ordinary way, chatting in every conceivable Spanish accent (and some murmur to each other in indigenous tongues I cannot identify) next to this Chilean-American born in Argentina as if nothing could be more natural?

How many of them are threatened with concentration camps and deportations and families sundered apart, how many of these compatriots of ours are adrift and in danger of living on the borders of legality? I dare not ask. But what is certain, what I can proclaim from the haven of this pungent paradise is that the men and women who make this country work, who build the houses and pave the roads, who clean the houses and cook the meals and care for the children, coming from every one of our twenty-one Latin American republics and meeting only here in *los Estados Unidos de América*, what I can unequivocally declare is that they are not going away.

Your wall, Señor Trump, has already been breached, your wall has already been defeated by our peaceful invasion.

Along with our food, we are here to stay.

Guests of the Holy Roman Empress
Maria Theresa

LEV GOLINKIN

An art museum is a great place to be a refugee. The authorities don't skimp on the heat, there are plenty of couches, loitering is encouraged for once (in a museum it's called "appreciating"), and everyone's so engrossed in the art, they don't look twice at what you're wearing. And if you allow yourself to get lost in the masterpieces, if you stand just long enough among incomprehensible murmurs in the soft, just-right lighting, you can forget that you're no longer part of the world. In a museum, no one cares. In a museum, everyone's a ghost.

Vienna's Kunsthistorisches Museum, where my father and I had gone during a slow afternoon in late February 1990, was a particularly magnificent choice of sanctuary. The crown jewel of a massive art collection amassed by the Hapsburgs, its gorgeous Baroque building proclaimed the power and glory of Vienna's bygone rulers, especially the eighteenth-century empress Maria Theresa.

"She was the quintessential benevolent despot," I'd heard another Soviet Jewish refugee proclaim during a long wait for asylum application interviews at the U.S. embassy in Vienna. The man went on to explain that benevolent despotism was born when divine right monarchies were inspired by the mores of the Enlightenment to leverage their powers in the service of society. I was nine years old, and had no idea what that meant, but the gist seemed to be that Maria Theresa liked art and also had armies which she used to make other people like art as well. A monumental statue of Maria sat outside the Kunsthistorisches Museum, arm extended toward the entrance as if to say, "I give you this. Now start appreciating."

It took Dad and I several reconnaissance trips to the museum before taking Maria up on her offer. At first, we satisfied ourselves with examining the facades; during another excursion, we made our way to the foyer. One afternoon, as a tour group was filing in, Dad gave me a light tap on the shoulder. "*Poshli*"—"Let's go"—said he, and we edged in around the crowd.

Maybe it was the malaise of a gray, late-winter afternoon, or some benevolent old decree from Maria instructing the guards to look the other way when financially strapped visitors came to the door, but Dad and I snuck in with ease. And yet, I remember that moment, for it was in that short walk across the black-and-white foyer that I felt myself become a refugee in a true and irreversible fashion.

The drastic images which make newsreels create the impression that people turn into refugees overnight. In my family's experience, that isn't true. Becoming a refugee is a gradual process, a bleaching out, a transition into a ghostly existence. With the exception of those born in refugee camps, every refugee used to have a life. It doesn't matter whether you were a physician in Bosnia or a goat herder in the Congo: what matters is that a thousand little anchors once moored you to the world. Becoming a refugee means watching as those anchors are severed, one by one, until at last you're floating outside of society, an untethered phantom in need of a new life.

Some strands are cut right away: Two months prior to winding up in Vienna, I had an address in Kharkov, Soviet

Ukraine, the same address I'd lived at my whole life. Three days and two international borders later, I was being herded by humanitarian workers speaking strange languages in a foreign train station, no longer a citizen of any nation, with no address to go back to and no addresses to seek out. Those are the anchors that snap overnight. Others erode more slowly.

It happens when your identity fades, names and titles giving way to numbers and papers. You become a visa to stamp, a pair of pupils for the quarantine doctor to check, fifty-five kilos to add to the maximum capacity of a train; at worst, an infestation, at best, a particle in transit. After a while, even your thoughts adjust to the new reality. It's the brutal little difference between subject and direct object. Once you've made the transition from When are we eating? to When are they feeding us? you know you're a refugee.

Your movements adjust, too, as you learn to be wary of the Westerners. The friendly shopkeeper let you warm up in the store yesterday, but maybe another refugee stole something this morning, and the threshold for kindness has been reached. Don't draw his attention—you're better off staying invisible. Within a couple of weeks, the eye contact rules become instinctual. Always stare when the humanitarian people are handing things out; supplies are limited, and you don't want to be behind the guy who gets the last one. Otherwise, don't stare at the locals, don't even look at the police, and never, ever approach young men with patches on their clothing.

Most Austrians barely noticed our existence; the young men with flags and patches who lounged on street corners and in metro stations were the opposite. They held themselves with absolute indifference to other Austrians, but stared, with unmistakable violence, at people who spoke strange tongues. Stay away from them—they love their homeland so much, they'll take that love out on refugees. Stay off the streets on Hitler's birthday (April 20), the humanitarian workers warned us. In fact, stay off the streets during all holidays. There's dangerous love in the air.

By the time Dad and I crossed the Kunsthistorisches Museum foyer into the rich green, red, and yellow galleries, all those lessons and more had long been absorbed. I'd already seen Dad hitchhike along Austrian roads, accept food from strangers, anxiously spit out pleas for asylum in front of bored clerks at the U.S. embassy. But all those things were necessary; they involved little choice. Our circumstances forced us to hitchhike to travel where we needed to go, to accept clothing handouts (the humanitarian workers gave us food, but clothing had to be scrounged up from local shelters), to plead with clerks to secure our resettlement. Sneaking into the museum was shocking because it was so brazenly optional. I never expected it from my strict father, who lived by the rules, even unnecessary ones.

Back in Ukraine, the trams of our city worked on a self-validating system: Instead of handing the wafer-thin tickets to the conductor, you punched them yourself, with blocky red hole punches mounted inside the tram. That was the idea, at least, but most passengers just kept their tickets to use for the next ride. I don't know the penalty for not validating, because in the countless times I'd ridden the tram, I never saw anyone caught. "We pretend to work, and they pretend to pay us," was the sarcastic unofficial motto of the rotting last years of the Soviet Union. No one checked. No one cared.

Dad always validated. During rush hour, when the trams were full, he'd pass the tickets to the passenger nearest the hole punch, tucking them into his coat upon return. If the tram was empty I'd tug on his sleeve, and he'd hoist me up by my armpits, so I could punch the tickets myself. He'd grown up clawing his way through the anti-Semitic Soviet system, the very system which eventually drove him to become a refugee in Austria, and he wasn't going to give it the satisfaction of copping a free ride. I didn't understand it at the time, of course, but I knew he always paid for his way, even when others didn't. Now, the memories of countless punched tickets floated through my mind, making Dad's decision to sneak into the museum even more jarring.

Maria Theresa's collection did not disappoint. Dad and I walked past an enormous marble statue of Theseus slaying the Minotaur, and took in the art, room by room, until we wound up in a large yellow hall with Bruegel paintings. I naturally ran to the fantastical works like the intricate *Tower of Babel*, but was surprised to find myself looking at the sedate landscapes as well. Children skated on a small village pond as a trio of hunters trudged home through the snow. Bakers wearing odd caps carried out large pies at a wedding feast. Peasants whirled to bagpipes, with a drunk reeling in the corner. It was all so vivid, both lifelike and strange, panels of bygone life preserved for the viewer.

Dad and I lingered in the Bruegel room until dusk was settling in. The young men with patches would soon start to congregate on street corners, and we had to make it back to the dilapidated old villa on the outskirts of the city, which the humanitarian people had converted into a refugee shelter. On the way through the museum foyer, Dad suddenly veered off for the gift shop, where he again surprised me by looking through its bewildering array of postcards. Window-shopping was safe, but handling goods broke another cardinal refugee rule: Be wary of breaking things you can't pay for, or being accused of stealing in a country where your legal status is questionable at best.

"We'll each pick two," Dad suddenly said. He chose a palace and a painting; I snatched up a statue of Maria Theresa, and a detailed Austro-Hungarian coat-of-arms. Whenever my parents allowed me to buy toys in Ukraine, I always examined and reexamined, carefully considering my options. Now, I barely glanced at the cards, hurriedly choosing before Dad changed his mind.

Dad paid for the postcards, then carefully stored them, along with the receipt, inside his large overcoat. "You have to act like a human being," he told me, tightening his sash and patting the coat to make sure the cards were secured. "*Ponimayesh?*" ("Understand?")

I wasn't sure whether I understood, but I said yes anyway. After months of only necessities, it felt wonderful to buy something, just because. I could almost feel the square little packet inside Dad's coat, giving us weight, making us more solid. "*Poshli,*" he tapped me, and out we went, past the ornate giant doors, past the outstretched arm of the benevolent despot Maria Theresa, back into Vienna, back to the world of ghosts.

The Parent Who Stays

REYNA GRANDE

Nobody had to tell me who the man sitting on my grand-mother's couch was. I'd grown up looking at his photograph hanging on our wall. He'd put on weight and wore glasses now. Instead of being black and white like in the photo, he was in color, his skin like rain-soaked earth.

I had to stand before this clean, well-fed stranger wearing a tattered dress, my head infested with lice, my belly swollen with tapeworm. I looked down at my dusty feet, the dirt caked under my toenails, my broken sandals held together by wire. "Go say hello to your father," my aunt said, pushing me toward him. All I wanted to do was run away.

He had left eight years before when I was two, and now he returned to find his children—me, my older brother and sister—just as he had left us: hungry, poor, vulnerable.

He hugged me too briefly, too hesitantly. And I realized that we were strangers to him, too.

This stranger, my father, had borrowed money from every-one he knew and hired a smuggler to take me and my siblings north to his home in the United States, where we were to begin a new life together. So, at the age of nine-and-a-half, I found myself at the U.S. border and became an "illegal" human being by cross-ing without permission for a chance to finally have a family.

I remember so vividly that moment when we were trying to cross, crawling through bushes, jumping over rocks, my body burning from the heat of the unforgiving sun and the white-hot fear inside me at the thought of being caught and losing my chance of having my father back in my life. At nine years old, I was too little to make the crossing, and I could not make my legs run fast enough. I prayed for wings.

Border patrol caught us and sent us back to Tijuana twice. It was a miracle that we made it the third time, although my father had to carry me on his back most of the way. It was there at the U.S. border where I got my first piggy-back ride from my father.

My parents didn't leave Mexico, they fled—not for their lives, but for life—seeking economic refuge from a country that couldn't or wouldn't give them the means to provide for their family. Mexico had failed them, and so they fled across the border to pursue the dream to give us a house and a better life.

Later I would come to learn that immigrant families who relocate together fare better than those who go through separation. Unfortunately, my family couldn't immigrate together. Financially, it wasn't possible. Legally, it wasn't feasible. We couldn't come here as "real" refugees. Poverty, no matter how extreme, doesn't meet any of the criteria for asylum. The term "economic refugee," a negative term here and in Europe, doesn't encourage compassion in the receiving country, either socially or politically.

Yet, what all displaced people have most in common, regardless of where we come from, regardless if we are "official" refugees or "illegal" immigrants, is our trauma. The trauma that propels us to this land, and the traumatic experiences that await us.

My first traumatic experience happened before I had the ability to remember. Due to a national debt crisis and subsequent peso devaluations, there were no jobs in Mexico, so in 1977 my father left his wife and children behind and became part of the largest wave of migration from Mexico ever, a wave that has only recently ended. I don't remember his departure. In my earliest memories, he was already gone. My identity as a little girl was that of a daughter with an absent father—a father I knew existed only through that black-and-white photograph. While he was away, our relationship was the empty space he'd left behind in my life.

Then the second trauma of my life occurred. I was four years old when I watched my mother walk away from me to go to the land across the border—*El Otro Lado*. I didn't know if I'd ever see her again. I stayed behind with relatives who didn't want me, who treated me as a burden and made me feel even more unloved and unwanted than I already felt.

My childhood was defined by the fear of being forgotten or abandoned, of being replaced by U.S.-born siblings.

As a child, I didn't understand why my parents had emigrated. I believed that they had left because they didn't love me enough either to stay with me or to take me with them.

Part of me didn't blame them for leaving. Though only a three-hour bus ride from Acapulco, my hometown is no beach resort. Iguala, Guerrero, isn't a place where you can thrive. You live a hand-to-mouth existence where all you think of is how to survive another day. Guerrero is the second poorest state in Mexico, with 70 percent of the population living in poverty. Due to the so-called "War on Drugs," it is also now the most violent state in Mexico, which is the second most violent country in the world. In 2016, there were twenty-three thousand homicides in Mexico, surpassed only by Syria, but our war—supported by the United States through the millions of dollars in funding, training of soldiers, and provisions of military aircraft, weapons, and vehicles to the Mexican government—isn't considered a "real" war, so Mexicans don't qualify for asylum. The United States considers persecution by a government a valid criterion for asylum, but not exploitation by criminal gangs or cartels.

Iguala is surrounded by the poppy fields that feed the U.S. drug epidemic, and the city bus station doubles as a distribution center for the cartels. Mexico supplies 90 percent of America's heroin, and Guerrero grows 50 percent of the poppies for the heroin trade. In this city of dirt roads and shacks, many locals survive by working in the poppy fields or in the U.S.-owned garment factory in my old neighborhood. The factory pays the workers $5 a day, but a pizza in Iguala will cost them $10. Iguala is also a place of special infamy—forty-three college students were taken and disappeared by the police working together with the cartel in 2014. To this day, we still don't know what happened to those students.

What sustained me through the years of separation from my parents was my dream of having a family again. I clung to it through the birthdays and Christmases, Mother's Days and Father's Days. I clung to it through the three attempts to cross the border and the drive along Interstate 5 to the front door of my father's home in Northeast Los Angeles.

I wish I could tell you that this is where and how my story ends, with this long-awaited reunification. With my siblings and me arriving at our father's house and starting a new life together in this great land of opportunity. I wish I could tell you that we got our happily-ever-after, and the trauma ended with the border crossing, and as soon as we overcame that barrier the psychological wounds began to heal. Unfortunately for us immigrants, the trauma doesn't end with a successful border crossing. I believe that for the rest of your life, you carry that border inside of you. It becomes part of your psyche, your being, your identity.

Even beyond being undocumented and fearing deportation and having to live in the shadows of society, was the dawning realization that there was a mismatch between how I had imagined my new home and the reality of how it actually was.

After so many years of separation, we didn't know each other. Though physically we had crossed the border, we'd missed so many years of each other's lives that emotionally and psychologically there was still a barrier between us. Immigration had turned my parents and me into strangers. The family I once had in Mexico no longer existed.

As time went on, the separation continued. As I grew up and assimilated, my assimilation became another barrier between me and my parents. When I learned English at the expense of Spanish, language increased the separation. The day I started junior high, I surpassed my parents, who had only gone to elementary school, and so my education further separated us.

Our emotions became a barrier as well. I was the daughter they left behind, and for most of my life, my relationship with my parents was filtered through that lens. Anger, resentment, and shame tainted how I saw them and interacted with them. My father dealt with his own psychological pain by drowning it in a can of Budweiser. Alcoholism helped him numb the suffering caused by his low-paying job, his limited English skills, his alienation in U.S. culture, but it also led him to a slow, painful death.

Thirty years would pass, and I would become a mother, wife, and successful writer. Yet when my father died in 2011, he was as much a stranger to me as he was when I first met him in my grandmother's home.

It is the central irony of my life that my parents emigrated to try to save our family, but by doing so, they destroyed it.

I know my experience isn't unique. Eighty percent of immigrant children in U.S. schools have been separated from their families during the process of migration. Complicated family dynamics add to the burden these children are already carrying, and schools that serve these children need to consider the trauma created by separation. Nothing is more counter-productive than the goal of rapid integration of immigrant and refugee children into the community. Assimilation and accul-turation add to their post-traumatic stress. Immigrant and refugee children need time, patience, love, and psychological help to heal from their experiences. Trauma follows them into the classroom as it did me, and powerfully affects performance and the ability to learn.

My education in U.S. schools was almost as traumatic as being abandoned by my parents. When I started fifth grade in Los Angeles, language was a barrier. Because I spoke no English, I was put at a corner table and ignored by my teacher. I felt voiceless. I sat in that corner, on the outside looking in, marginalized, excluded, "othered." Months went by, and for my teacher, it was as if I didn't exist.

Once I learned English, I still felt invisible when the books given to me by my teachers and the librarians had nothing to do with my experience. While I was fascinated by books such as Sweet Valley High, which gave me a glimpse to a world that wasn't mine—white, middle-class America—I knew that life could never be mine. Through the years, I'd often wonder, *Where am I in these stories?* Invisibility became another barrier to overcome.

At thirteen years old, I understood that I would have to write my way into existence.

Growing up, however, I didn't know I was traumatized. I didn't have the words to describe what I felt: anxiety, depression, post-traumatic stress disorder. These words weren't part of my vocabulary, so I never used them—I described my feelings through stories.

And yet, I know I was lucky. If I arrived at the border today seeking asylum, I would have the door slammed in my face. I would be told that I haven't suffered enough, that I should go back to my country and suffer some more. Even if I was seeking refuge, I was not a refugee.

Three years ago, there was a surge in unaccompanied child immigrants, most from Central America, who came seeking refuge from poverty, oppression, and violence created by criminal gangs. Their migration continues, though their arrival at the border is no longer in record numbers because the United States is now paying Mexico to catch and deport these children before they reach the border. But for the ones who do arrive in the United States, after all the trauma they've endured in their countries and during the long journey to the border, they're thrown into detention centers and forced to face federal immigration judges to plead their cases in court, often without legal representation.

At nine-and-a-half years old, the same age my daughter is now, I broke U.S. law and became a "criminal" for daring to aspire to a better future. I ran across the border seeking refuge from abandonment, desperate to leave behind me those feelings of being unwanted and unloved. Once across, I thought I was done with borders; I didn't know there would be more. Yet, in the past thirty-two years that I've lived in this country, I've had to cross cultural, language, legal, gender, and career barriers, and more.

Writing continues to be an act of survival. As an immigrant or refugee, there is no end to trauma. You're always the object of hostile acts and political rhetoric that accuses you of being a criminal and a rapist. And it takes a toll. But I'm grateful that my experience was not as grueling and horrific as that of those coming today. Unlike these new immigrants and refugees, I did not experience the terrors of war; I did not have any family members killed or disappeared by criminal gangs or *narcos*; I did not have a gun put to my head to force me to join a gang. I did not travel alone to the border: I did not ride the deadly train, *La Bestia*, across Mexico; I was not robbed; I was not raped; I was not attacked by gangs, bandits, or corrupt Mexican officials along the way. I was not a victim of sex trafficking or child labor.

I was a victim of a consequence of migration that is often overlooked or given little importance—the psychological violence of watching your family fall apart. Family separation and disintegration is the price my family paid for a shot at the American Dream.

My story in the United States was full of abuse and instability, and it was hard to find my way in this country, to try to earn my right to remain and find a place to belong, but lucky for me, I finally did. Under an amnesty signed by Ronald Reagan, my family became legal residents, and eventually U.S. citizens. Despite psychological and emotional distress, I went to college and became the first in my family to get a university diploma. I became a teacher, a published author, a homeowner. I have won awards. I married a good man and have two beautiful children. I accomplished every goal I set for myself and have been more than lucky.

With children of my own, I have come to understand my father in a way I could not have before. I look at my children and try to imagine what it would be like to leave them, to walk away from them because I cannot provide for them. I look at my nine-year-old daughter and try to imagine endangering her life by taking her across the U.S. border. Would my own child survive what I survived? I don't know. What I do know is that if I were put in my father's place, I would do the same. I would risk everything for my children.

I bear witness every day to the trauma of our loss, suffering wounds that will never heal. It's a price I would pay a hundred times over because one of my father's greatest gifts to me, and indirectly to his grandchildren, is this: His decision to immigrate has allowed me to be the parent he could never be. Unlike him, I will never be a stranger to my children.

I now get to be the parent who stays.

To Walk in Their Shoes

MERON HADERO

What my mother most remembers about becoming a refugee is a sign that hung in an interim shelter in West Berlin that said, "A refugee is a person without a country." This was painful to her, and plainly incorrect; she had a country, even if she had to leave it behind. I don't think it occurred to her then that ours was a one-way trip.

My father remembers the global nature of that experience. The Polish, Cambodian, and Afghan refugees who were our neighbors in West Berlin, the Vietnamese refugees who lived with us in the Abraham Welcome House in Washington, D.C., a whole population of exiles from around the world, sharing this experience of fleeing to or fleeing from, taking a leap of faith toward some place hopeful and away from some place unbearable.

I remember almost nothing from that time. Having reached Germany when I was two and leaving several months after my third birthday, I was just approaching that age when substantive memories are starting to form, but when they often don't quite yet take hold. Still, the first glimpses of my remembered life start there in Germany; my remembered life began in that time of becoming and being a refugee.

I was born in Addis Ababa, Ethiopia, to two parents who were both established physicians. The Ethiopian empire had

crumbled years before and had given way to a brutal communist junta. I was born in the waning days of the "red terror,"
the bloody, ruthless repression of the opposition in the country.
Many in my family were detained, an aunt was disappeared, an
uncle executed. My parents struggled to schedule their wedding, hoping for better days and the perfect moment, but life
had to go on.

I was too young to remember Ethiopia then. Nor do I
remember taking a plane from Addis Ababa with my father to
be with my mother in Quedlinburg, East Germany, where she
had won a grant to do medical research. And I don't remember how my father had managed, after many failed attempts, to
get permission for us to travel abroad. It was a lucky break that
my father is certain came just in the nick of time in the form
of three visas to what was then Czechoslovakia. The guards at
Checkpoint Charlie let us all pass into West Berlin even though
we were supposed to be traveling east.

I don't remember waiting outside the gates of the U.S. con-
sulate that same evening, asking if we could go to America, nor
do I remember one of the consular staff coming to see us, or that
as the Christmas fireworks exploded, my father feared we had
found our way to another war zone.

I don't remember that my mother prayed and fretted and
did everything she could to get my baby sister out of Ethiopia,
where she had to stay behind. I don't remember yet another
complicated plan taking shape; that to get the right paperwork,
we had to pretend that my aunt was her mother, someone else
her father. When their plane from Addis Ababa to Paris refu-
eled in Frankfurt and they walked off to join us there, I don't
remember my mother's heart breaking when my sister didn't

remember us anymore; we were unrecognizable to her after just several months apart.

Besides my family, what I remember about those early days as a refugee is living in Düsseldorf, where we were sent after Berlin, and, specifically, I remember my friend there, Justyna. That happens sometimes: A place is really remembered as a person, or a person is remembered as a place. Though we'd never see each other again, my friendship with Justyna, a simple childhood friendship with regular playdates and ordinary kindness, was a source of stability and certainty in days when those were in such short supply.

And after that, after we moved to Washington, D.C., I remember well that my father's old professor, who had been in Ethiopia teaching abroad, took us in. And we lived with his family in Cedar Rapids, Iowa, and built a new life from there.

. . .

In 2013, I received a travel grant from the University of Michigan to retrace the emigration route from Ethiopia to Quedlinburg to Berlin to Düsseldorf. I was given the chance to know what it felt like to take that trip as an adult, to see if any of it felt familiar, to see if I could somehow coax the past out of the shadows and into the light. It would be a chance to pull back the curtains and see if the room wasn't so empty after all. I was around the age my parents had been when they completed that journey all those years ago, and so I set out on a pilgrimage to walk in their shoes, to put myself in their place, as best I could. And I wanted to feel more a part of the story, which I often thought of as belonging to my parents, who have always been its narrators. They were the ones who remembered, who told, who chose what was revealed and what should be withheld. But in going back, I was positioning myself a bit closer to the center, which felt a little uncomfortable, but accurate; I was there, too. This was my story, too. After starting in Ethiopia, which I've visited relatively often as an adult, I flew into Frankfurt and took a train through the eastern part of Germany to Quedlinburg.

Quedlinburg is a town so small and obscure that many Germans I asked didn't know where it was, not even at the tourism office in the airport. Quedlinburg looks almost staged, a pristine medieval German castle town in the East. It's also a UNESCO World Heritage site, a classification that requires historical preservation, a certain fidelity to the past, a certain valuation of the past over the present. Quedlinburg was largely untouched by World War II (whereas Dresden, only a two-hour drive away, was flattened), and it has been largely untouched by modernization. It does have a "new town," but I'm told it was built around the twelfth century. If any place should have been easily remembered, it would be one as unchanging as this.

I spent days walking through the town, eventually renting an English language audio tour, and even when I fell out of step with it, the tour never felt out of sync as it described one medieval building, then the next. The only real grounding detail I clung to was that there had been a language school where my mother had studied German, living with students from around the communist world—Ethiopia, Angola, Nicaragua, Cuba, Eastern Europe—but no one I spoke with had been aware of it, or at least, no one admitted to it. (I heard a little about it again when I visited the Stasi Archive in Berlin, where an archivist knew of it. "Of course," he said. Quedlinburg may be a well-preserved town, but it's nothing next to the perfect recall of that vast, vast archive.) In all, what felt most overpowering there was a sense of wonder, not so much of the lovely little town, but of my mother, who came here from the developing world—her first time out of the country—and landed alone in East Germany in the dead of winter without the things she loved, and missing Addis Ababa, her children, her whole family, her house, the warmth, everything.

I went to Berlin next, familiar because, I think, it was not my first time back. When I asked my parents about the difficulties they had encountered there, I uncovered stories I never knew, how we were reviled and resented by some of the strangers we lived among, how a new sense of unsafety sprung up from such encounters. My parents had tried to let go of these difficulties in the intervening years. They didn't talk about them. They preferred to focus on what they will always see as a lucky story, considering what might have been.

When I asked my mother and father if there was anything specific I should look up in Berlin, my mother said, of Berlin itself, she especially remembered the Zoological Garten. My father sent an email, an outpouring. He told me how to retrace our steps: Maybe I could find the pension with the sweet owner where we first had a room before all of our money ran out, or the charity that ultimately settled us in, or our temporary home on Friedrichstrasse (he said the address was either 150 or 15, but when I walked along the road as the numbers got higher, I saw that 150 was near the fancy shops, so it must have been 15, an aging, graffitied building in what seemed to be an immigrant neighborhood in an unassuming part of town).

Throughout the city, I walked amid the Berlin Wall in pieces, portions even lined up like giant dominoes. I waited to see whether memory would push through whatever blockades there may be in my mind; I waited for the wall to come down. Though all around, there was the industry of memory, where loud tour guides talked above each other to huddled groups who followed them on Segway or bike or foot to hear stories, none of these recollections were my own.

When Germany was divided, West Berlin was an island in East Germany, so when my family left for Düsseldorf, 366 miles away, the only way out was not through, but over—by plane. We went to Hanover first, spent a night there, then took a train to Düsseldorf. This time, I flew direct. When I got to Düsseldorf, I realized I now felt totally at ease in Germany, and I wondered if that feeling itself was a form of memory, some sense of relief hidden somewhere in my muscles or bones, because, by the time we got here, our family had been united. We lived in a small home with a stipend and felt slightly more settled.

When I walked around Düsseldorf, I looked a little more closely at the women who were around my age—perhaps I would somehow recognize Justyna there, or she me. More so, especially when I went to Schwarzer Weg, the street on which my father said we lived. My mother didn't remember the address, but my father thought he did. They both remembered it being in Benrath, a small borough in town. I took a taxi to the address my father had given me, but it led nowhere, and the taxi drove around in circles, one way, then the other. My taxi driver had been born in Turkey, and he said that as an adult, he had gone back to see his childhood home. He said he had an experience like the one he was driving me to, and he seemed excited to be on this journey with me. But maybe he was thrilled that we were on this wild goose chase, wandering aimlessly for so long, the fare climbing and climbing.

We didn't find the exact address, but came upon a stretch of road just off Schwarzer Weg, a little street that looked familiar. I remembered not the place, but a photograph: me, two blond boys, and Justyna were standing outside an apartment complex, looking up playfully from our game. In the background, I remember brick buildings with tan balconies. Here were brick buildings with tan balconies. It was not the kind of on-the-nose confirmation I was looking for, but I didn't mind. As I told my parents about that discovered road in the borough of Benrath, as I told them what Düsseldorf was like now—the cluster of Frank Gehry buildings along the Rhine, the posters of Tina Turner, perhaps one of the most famous immigrants in neighboring Cologne—I felt myself becoming a voice in this story, too. They asked me questions, they wanted to know what it looked like there, what it felt like. What memories of mine, of theirs, of any of ours, I could confirm or refine. They were surprised to hear that the parts of Berlin that had been in the GDR were arty and chic, and sad to learn that the East felt separate and closed off, the windows in the train stations broken, a sense of wanting showing through.

. . .

There is a link between Addis Ababa, Quedlinburg, Berlin, Düsseldorf, and the United States. At least, for a few people in the world, these cities are connected, and I think of all the routes of emigration taken by refugees like us, routes that have been carved into memory, into family stories. Along these paths are friends lost, debts that can never be repaid, kindnesses that can't possibly be returned, promises and hopes broken, slights and affronts that are hard to forget or say aloud, places of refuge filled with people who bravely come together from all corners, moving from place to place, looking for safety, for community, for home.

God's Fate

ALEKSANDAR HEMON

The world is full of people who left the place where they were born just to stay alive, and then to die in a place where they never expected to live. The world is sown with human beings who did not make it here, wherever that may be, though they might be on their way. Many Bosnians, and I am one of them, made it here. In my case, the here I call my own is Chicago, where I ended up in 1992, at the beginning of the war that would make Bosnia known for all the wrong and terrible reasons. I've written books featuring that experience, and they were published, so I followed them around the world, where I ran into other Bosnians: Miami, Tokyo, London, Stockholm, Toronto, Paris, You Name It. I also have family in Canada, the UK, France, Italy, Sweden, Australia, etc. Bosnians are one of the many refugee nations: Roughly one quarter of the country's pre-war population is now displaced, scattered all over the globe. There is no Bosnian without a family member living elsewhere, which is to say that displacement would be essential to the national character if such a thing actually existed.

Each time I meet a Bosnian, I ask: "How did you get here?" The stories they tell me are often long, fraught with elisions, edited by the presence of the many new-life-in-the-new-land modalities. People get overwhelmed while telling them, remember things they didn't know they could or would want to remember, insist on details that are both extremely telling and irrelevant, soaked with not always apparent meanings. Entire histories are inscribed in each story, whole networks of human lives and destinies outlined. Migration generates narratives; each displacement is a tale; each tale unlike any other. The journeys are long and eventful, experiences accumulated, lives reevaluated and reconfigured, worlds torn down and recreated. Each getting here is a narrative entanglement of memory and history and emotions and pain and joy and guilt and ideas undone and reborn. Each story contains everything I've ever cared about in literature and life, mine or anyone else's. Each story complements all the other ones—the world of refugees is a vast narrative landscape.

The recent upsurge in bigotry directed at migrants and refugees is predictably contingent upon their dehumanization and deindividualization—they are presented and thought of as a mass of nothings and nobodies, driven, much like zombies, by an incomprehensible, endless hunger for what "we" possess, for "our" life. In Trumpist America, they are not only denied, but also punished for that perceived desire.

But each person, each family, has their own history, their own set of stories that define them and locate them in the world, their own networks of love and friendship and suffering, their own human potential. To reduce them to a faceless mass, to deprive them of their stories is a crime against humanity and history. What literature does, or at least can do, is allow for individual narrative enfranchisement. The very proposition of storytelling is that each life is a multitude of details, an irreplaceable combination of experiences, which can be contained in their totality only in narration. I take it to be my writerly duty to facilitate the telling of such stories.

Which is why I went to North Carolina in the spring of 2017 and talked to a man named Kemalemir Frashto. This is the much-shortened version of the story he told me.

When the war in Bosnia started in 1992, his name was Kemal Frašto, and he was eighteen years old. He lived with his parents and brothers in Foča, a town in eastern Bosnia, best known for its prison, among the largest and the most notorious ones in the former Yugoslavia. Foča is on the river Drina, close to the border with Serbia and Montenegro, and was thus of strategic value. On April 4, 1992, the Frašto family prayed at their mosque in celebration of Eid, unaware that the war was about to start. That day, all the prisoners were released from the prison, and an enormous murder of crows flew up into the blue sky. On April 8, the Serb forces began an all-out attack and takeover of Foča, detaining the people of Muslim background. After establishing full control, the Serbs blew up all the mosques in town, including the sixteenth-century Aladža mosque. Two of Kemal's older brothers managed to escape with their families to Sarajevo. But Kemal's father refused to leave, because he "had no argument with anybody." Kemal and his brother Emir, nine years older, remained with their parents, only to be placed under house arrest. Serb volunteers and paramilitaries frequently and randomly came by to threaten and abuse them, and would've likely killed them if it wasn't for one of their Serb neighbors, who stayed with them day and night to make sure they were safe. But that arrangement couldn't last, as their protector's life was thus also endangered. Eventually, a group of

Serb paramilitaries caught them alone; one of them, Kemal's schoolmate, raped his mother. For weeks the brothers bore witness to the killing in their neighborhood: one day Kemal watched helplessly as his neighbor was slaughtered on the spot, while his wife was repeatedly raped, whereupon her rapists cut her breasts off. Eventually, Kemal and his brother were arrested and taken to the old prison which now served as a concentration camp for Muslim men.

Foča was ethnically cleansed rapidly and with exceptional brutality. The Drina carried schools of corpses, rape camps were set up all over town. Kemal and Emir shared a small cell with other men, all of them beaten and humiliated regularly. The chief torturer was their neighbor Zelja. He told the men he tortured that they'd be spared if they crossed themselves and expressed their pride in being Serbs. Kemal and Emir refused—they had lived as Muslims, and they would die as Muslims. Besides, those who complied were killed anyway. One day, Zelja broke Emir's teeth and Kemal's cheek bone. Another day, a guard broke Kemal's arm with a gun butt, the bone sticking out. When, in June 1992, Emir was "interrogated" again, alone this time, Kemal could hear his brother's begging for mercy: "Don't, Zelja! What did I ever do to you? What do we need this for?" "So that you can see what it's like when Zelja beats you," the tormentor responded. Emir never returned to the cell, and Kemal never saw him again.

Zelja would be tried and sentenced in The Hague for war crimes and rape. He served his sentence, and returned to Foča, as the Dayton Peace Accord awarded the town to the Serbs, thus effectively rewarding them for their atrocities. After the war, Kemal delegated a local friend to ask Zelja for information that could help him find his brother's remains. Zelja demanded 20,000 KM (about $10,000) to tell him where Emir's remains were, and Kemal neither thought that he should pay up nor had the money. "I'm not a killer. It's not for me to punish him. God will do that," Kemal says. "All I want is to find my brother." (Not so long ago, he finally received a tip about the place where his brother's remains were dumped, and managed to arrange a proper Muslim burial for him.)

Kemal remained in prison for eighteen months, alternating between wanting to survive and hoping to die. While imprisoned, a Serb friend of Emir's sent her boyfriend, Zoka, to find Kemal in the camp and bring him to their home for a shower and dinner. But Zoka ended up attracted to Kemal. Next time, he picked him up from the prison without telling his girlfriend and they ended up having sex. This happened more than once, and Zoka returned him to prison each time. Kemal was in closeted denial throughout his adolescence, so he lost his virginity with Zoka, the awkward intercourse with a girl forced upon him by his oldest brother notwithstanding. He now sees the sexual experience with Zoka as God-sent, something that helped him not lose his mind in the camp.

In November 1993, there was heavy fighting near Foča and the Serb forces used the prisoners as human shields. Kemal was one of the bodies the Serbs put up in front of their positions to shoot over their heads. The desperate Bosnians deployed a multiple rocket launcher to hit Serb trenches; an explosion lifted Kemal and threw him into a ditch, where he lay unconscious for a while. When he came to, he didn't appear to be injured. It was dark, and there was no one around—not even dead and wounded—except for a beautiful, barefoot man in a white robe, emanating a kind of interior light. For a moment, Kemal thought he'd reached heaven and was facing Allah, but the man said to Kemal: "Let's go."

"Where am I going?" Kemal asked.

"To Sarajevo," the man said.

Sarajevo was under siege at the time, and at least fifty miles away. Kemal walked for seven nights and six days; at night, the man in the white robe lit up the path for Kemal. He was a *melek* (an angel), Kemal realized, guiding him through a difficult mountainous terrain and away from combat zones. Kemal subsisted on what he foraged: wild garlic and tree leaves and carrots from abandoned gardens. At one point, he nearly stumbled upon a Serb convoy; hidden in the bushes and terrified, he watched tanks thunder by sixty yards away from him. The melek consoled him, assuring him it was not yet his time to die.

Taking a long roundabout way, Kemal reached the hills above Sarajevo, where he ran into an elderly *četnik*. By this time, Kemal had a long beard, which is part of the četnik appearance, so the old man assumed he was one of them. The četnik asked him where he was coming from. At that moment, what popped in Kemalemir's head was Little Red Riding Hood (*Crvenkapica*), perhaps because the old četnik's beard gave him a wolf-like appearance. Kemalemir said he was taking food to his grandmother, which the old četnik commended. Below them, in the valley, Sarajevo was in flames. The četnik said to Kemal: "Sarajevo is burning. Fuck their Muslim mothers, we're going to get them!"

Kemal walked on and reached the Bosnian defensive positions on the outskirts of the city. He had a četnik beard, no uniform or documents, nor could he read the Bosnian Army ranks (as it'd been founded while he'd been in prison), so the Bosnians had no way of knowing who he was, what army he might belong to. Before he passed out, he only managed to utter: "I'm exhausted. I'm Muslim. I come from Foča."

The phrase *Božja sudbina* (God's fate) is common in Bosnian, and it's different from *Božja volja* (God's will). I don't know the theological underpinning of the difference, but I suspect that God's fate implies a plan, a predestined trajectory laid down by God for each of us to move along without His having to do much else about it; in contrast, God's will has an interventionist quality, and might be subject to His whims. Be that as it may, Kemal claims that it was God's fate that his cousin was a soldier in the Bosnian unit that captured him so that he could vouchsafe for Kemal and stop the short-fused soldiers from killing him. Kemal therefore ended up attached to an infusion pouch in a hospital in Sarajevo. He weighed eighty-eight pounds. The melek appeared to him only one more time, a few weeks later, in a dream, only to implore him not to talk about what happened to anybody.

In 1994, with the help of a CB radio operator, Kemal managed to get in touch with his parents, who subsequently found a way to besieged Sarajevo to be with their son. After witnessing terrible crimes and surviving, they'd crossed the border in Montenegro, Kemal's father hiding under his wife's skirt. In Montenegro, Kemal's mother had discovered she was pregnant from the rape and underwent an abortion. When they reached Sarajevo, it was discovered that she had a tumor in her uterus. When it was taken out, it weighed eleven pounds.

Kemal spent the rest of the war in and around Sarajevo. He surreptitiously slept with men, including a fellow member of the mosque choir, with whom he'd meet to study the Quran. In 1995, he got a degree in Oriental studies and Arabic language at the University of Sarajevo. In 1996, desperate to leave Bosnia, he went to Ludwigsburg, near Stuttgart, where his oldest brother lived. At the time, the German government, having determined that the war in Bosnia was over and that it was safe to return, emptied all the refugee camps, sending the Bosnians back. Kemal entered Germany illegally and found a job as a stripper at a (straight) bar. He enjoyed working there, as did his German lady clients, who wallpapered his sweaty body with money. He discovered and explored the very active gay scene in Cologne. At a local swimming pool, for the first time ever, he saw two men holding hands and kissing, publicly in love.

But he felt he had to go back home, even if his pockets were lined with money. God's people lived in Bosnia, he believed, while Germany was populated with sinners. Soon upon his return to Sarajevo, he met Belma; they got married ten days later. The marriage was supposed to counter his terrible desires; he never cheated on his wife, but kept imagining men while having sex with her. He considered himself to be sick and abnormal, and kept trying to do what was expected from a "normal" man. Belma even got pregnant, but then had a miscarriage; Kemal was relieved, because the drop in hormone levels meant she lost interest in sex.

He needed a job, but his Oriental Studies and Arabic Language degree wasn't going to get him anywhere. One winter day, after Sarajevo was swamped with snow, he went to the unemployment office to look for work, and a woman there asked him if he'd be willing to shovel. He was, and he shoveled the streets with enough enthusiasm to be offered a full-time job at Sarajevo

City Services. Come spring, he was given a bicycle and a broom and assigned to the former Olympic Village, where the international athletes used to stay during the 1984 Winter Olympics. It was a good job, until his boss called him into his office to express his shock at the fact that Kemal had a college degree. Then he promptly fired him for being overqualified.

This was a turning point for Kemal. He announced to Belma that he was determined to leave Bosnia. At first she wouldn't even consider joining him, but then changed her mind. They applied for an American resettlement visa, went through a series of interviews, and waited anxiously for a response. After two years or so, they were invited for their final interview in Split, Croatia. Kemal's English was not good, but he understood when the interviewer asked: "What would you do if I told you that you have failed this interview?" Kemal said: "If you open that window, I'll jump out of it right now."

In 2001, they resettled in Utica, New York, where Bosnian refugees were nearly a quarter of the population. Kemal worked at an enormous casino, and also as a cook at an Italian restaurant. He was often suicidal, and exhausted himself with work, sometimes clocking twenty hours. But this is how life often works: in the middle of a mind-crushing depression, he and Belma went to Las Vegas, where he won $16,000 on a slot machine. He used that money to buy his first American house.

By 2003, he could no longer stand the pretense of "normal" life, and came out to his wife by way of deliberately leaving gay porn images on his computer. Belma was furious, and exacted revenge by telling every Bosnian she knew that her husband was gay, falsely claiming that he was HIV positive. The casino employed hundreds of Bosnians, and most of them now shunned him. Nonetheless, he worked out a divorce deal with Belma, from which she got enough money to move to Finland and take up with a man she had met on the internet. It turned out that the man was a human trafficker, who locked her up and forced her into sexual servitude. She went through hell, escaping and returning to the United States only with Kemal's help.

Kemal went back to school, attained a diploma of a radiography technician. At the local mosque he met a Dr. Kahn, who told him that his desires were not sinful because God made him as he was. Kemal also met Tim, an American, and they became very close, well beyond being occasional lovers, eventually moving in together. On becoming a U.S. citizen in 2005, Kemal merged his first name with his dead brother's so they can always be together, his legal name now Kemalemir Preston Frashto.

When Kemalemir found a job in North Carolina, where he moved with Tim in 2007, it seemed that things were going well. But, as many refugees know, it's exactly when things seem to be going well that post-traumatic stress disorder kicks in full force. Frequently suicidal, Kemal went from therapist to therapist—one told him that he was making stuff up, another came drunk to sessions—until he found a Muslim one, who helped him see that he was not abnormal, neither a sinner nor a monster. Kemal began reconciling his faith with his sense of himself, his innermost feelings with Islam. He understood that God created those feelings, as He created his body and its desires. Despite all that, in the summer of 2013 he attempted to "pass the final judgment upon himself" as the Bosnian idiom (*sam sebi presuditi*) would have it: While Tim was at work, Kemal strung a rope on the staircase and climbed the chair. As Kemalemir kicked off the chair, Tim walked in—God's fate, again—just in time to cut the rope.

What would complete Kemal's salvation was love. He'd been corresponding by way of Facebook with Dženan, a Sarajevo hairdresser in a sham marriage with a lesbian. Kemal traveled back to Bosnia to meet Dženan in person, not expecting much more than a good time, something that could get him out of his PTS doldrums. But when they met for the first time at a bus stop in Vogošća, a drab Sarajevo suburb, they embraced and didn't let go of each other for a very long time. It felt as though they'd known each other for years, and their love grew fast. They had a great time together, and as soon as Kemalemir returned to North Carolina, he began thinking of his next visit to Sarajevo. Even so, they couldn't quite imagine a life together; at the very least, it was logistically complicated.

When Kemalemir returned to Bosnia around Thanksgiving the same year, he devised a simple plan where Dženan, who got a U.S. tourist visa in the meantime, would accompany him back to Charlotte, stay illegally if need be, so they could see how things between them would develop. But by this time, Dženan's wife, nicknamed Rambo, became unwilling to let go of her sham husband and started creating problems, as did her family. Her father asked to be repaid the money he'd spent on the wedding; her sister remembered that Dženan owed her 50 KM ($25), and even Rambo declared that if Dženan wanted a divorce it would cost him $1,000. Dismayed by the ugliness of the situation, they paid up and left earlier than planned.

Soon upon the arrival to North Carolina they decided to get married, which would not just confirm their mutual commitment, but also resolve Dženan's immigration status. Gay marriage was not legal in North Carolina at the time, so they went to Maryland and got married on June 12, 2014.

Until he got married, Kemalemir stayed away from the Charlotte-area Bosnians. But with marriage, he felt a need to engage with the community. He started going to the Bosnian mosque, became active and involved in the community despite their homophobia, ranging from elbow-nudging and snickering to outright insults. Kemalemir and Dženan also wanted to become registered members of the Bosnian mosque, which would, among other things, guarantee them a proper religious burial. They believed they were a legitimate part of the Bosnian Muslim community, and that there could be no viable reason why they should not be members. Some reasonable people in the community suggested to the imam that the issue be passed upward; it was eventually referred all the way back to Bosnia to be considered by a council of muftis, who then referred it back to the imam, thus completing the vicious circle. The donation Dženan and Kemal gave to the mosque was refused, their membership application denied. The imam told them that the application might have been approved had they not been so open. Kemalemir separates faith and religion and believes that, while faith comes directly from God, religion comes from man. Dženan is the love of his life, and he cannot see how God could object to that.

In the meantime, Donald Trump got elected. "I'm Muslim, refugee, gay," Kemalemir says. "A perfect target for Trump." After their marriage, Dženan had a temporary green card, which made them worry about the possibility of deportation, until a permanent status was approved in the winter of 2017.

Uncomfortable though they may be in Trump's America, they think it was God's fate that they ended up here, and together.

. . .

Kemalemir told me all this, and much more, at his small apartment in Charlotte. He sat on a comfortable leather sofa facing a huge TV with programs broadcasting live from Bosnia. Next to the TV, there were pictures of the Kemalemir and Dženan grinning, a black-and-white photo of Emir, and a plaque reading:

If Tears Could Build a Stairway
And Memories a Lane
I'd Walk Right up to Heaven
And Bring You Home Again

There was also a dark carved-wood corner in the dining area which Kemalemir had bought from an Iranian who at first didn't want to sell it at any price. A few hundred years old, the wooden corner was populated with *ibriks*, pitchers with curved spouts, and other Bosnian-style mementos. On the round table next to it, there was an intricate beige tablecloth, crocheted by Kemalemir's mother.

In 2000, Kemal visited Foča for the first time after the war and for the last time before going to America. His former neighbors, the mother and sister of the Serb neighbor who protected his family at the beginning of it all, insisted he stop by for lunch, as they might never see each other again. When he stepped into the house, he recognized much of his family furniture: cabinets, armoires, tables. The plates the lunch was served on also used to belong to the Fraštos. "How come you have all this?" he asked the mother, if rhetorically. He knew that, after his family fled, the neighbors took furniture and other household items, claiming that if they hadn't, someone else would have taken them. During the lunch, Kemalemir had to swallow his hurt and anger, because, he says, his mother always taught him to be the better person. But on the way out the sister, no doubt feeling guilty, said to her mother: "Give him something that belonged to them, as a souvenir," and the mother gave him the crocheted tablecloth.

In Charlotte, Kemalemir showed me the circular area where his mother had used white thread when she'd run out of the beige kind. The shift in the color was so subtle I would've never noticed if he hadn't pointed it out it to me. "This thing, this small thing," he said, "is what makes it unique."

Second Country

JOSEPH KERTES

When the Hungarians surprised the Russians by rising up against them in the fall of 1956, the borders opened and my family fled. I was almost five. We left behind us our relatives and friends, our comfortable home in Budapest, our possessions (except for what we could carry), our language, our culture, a thousand years of history, and these last memories. I saw a Hungarian soldier hanging from a lamppost, and he was staring right at me, as I was at him, but he could no longer see. He would remain a constant reminder that we still had our lives. And a chance for freedom lay ahead.

We ran like mad, hundreds of us. We ran by foot by night across the frontier into Austria. Bombs kept going off, and my brother and I would stop to look up, but there were no planes dropping them. My brother kept asking what was going on, and no one answered. It was not until we'd crossed the border that we found out we'd been running across a minefield. But my father kept urging us on in the darkness, and he kept telling us we were the lucky ones, but I was young. I kept looking behind me and wondering who the unlucky ones might have been and hoping, possibly, that we still might go home to join them. But then the vision of the hanging soldier loomed up over me, kept me running onward.

We arrived at last at a single lamppost, shining brightly in the darkness, and my father told us, "This is Austria." I remember thinking what a crappy country we'd come to. We left home for this? This solitary lamppost?

We were uncertain as to where we were headed ultimately, so my grandmother had taken opera records with her, not knowing when she would hear her favorite music again. (My father was so angry with his mother on account of the weight of her bag that he broke a couple of her records on the pedestal of that Austrian lamppost.) My mother had taken old photographs and a few recent ones of my brother and me as babies, plus a few memorabilia. We might as well have been anticipating Tim O'Brien's *The Things They Carried*. My father had taken only valuables: gold jewelry and gold coins. My older brother (two and a half years older) carried fighting toys: spurs and a gun in a holster, both of which looked real, and a bullet belt with what looked like real bullets, in case we made it all the way to the Wild West. I had a chocolate marzipan bar, some tin soldiers which my brother also liked, and a sheriff's badge my brother said I could carry and keep.

Though harried and apprehensive, we nevertheless felt safe outside our homeland. For us, our homeland had a sad history. My mother had lost both her parents and six of her siblings in World War II. My father had lost his only sibling, his only brother. And now what we hadn't lost to the Germans during World War II, we lost or left behind for the Russians. The idea of "ownership" became fluid. The Russians had liberated Hungary from the Germans, but they never left. They squatted on Hungary, and the West left them to it, as they had with Poland and Czechoslovakia. Stalin had shrewdly allied himself with the West to defeat Hitler, and now he quietly and unobtrusively gobbled up the nations he had liberated—unobtrusively at least until this brief revolution in Hungary. When the larger-than-life statue of Papa Stalin that had stood in Heroes' Square in Budapest came crashing down at the hands of the rebels in 1956, all the ironies came crashing down with it. (Stalin was larger-than-life in every respect—demonic at the best of times—but smaller-than-life in actual stature. Like Hitler. Like Napoleon.)

Standing at the Austrian lamppost, we were now free, free from the clutches of our conquerors and oppressors. So now what? We made our way by bus to Vienna, the bus loaded with Hungarian refugees like us, and we were taken to a large army barracks, which the Austrians had set up for us. We were tested for illness, inoculated and disinfected with sprays and ointments. We were given a good meal, plus chocolates. Then the big question to follow on "So now what?" was "So where to?"

This decision was critical for my family, and we appreciated that we had a choice at all. My Jewish family had no such options during World War II. And famously, or infamously, Jews trying to flee Europe in 1939 aboard the German liner the *St. Louis*, from Hamburg, Germany, were turned away in Cuba, then Miami, and sailed back to Europe where most perished. In another instance, Rudolf Kastner, a Jewish Hungarian lawyer, had arranged with Adolf Eichmann that, for a certain amount of money, the German commander would allow 1,600 Jews to escape to Switzerland. The selection process was ruthless in that the determining factor was money and money alone. Most who couldn't afford to pay perished. (Some six hundred thousand Hungarian Jews perished.)

Then along came the Soviets, deftly swallowing one country after another the way the Third Reich had wanted to. The West must have felt guilty, so they opened their doors to us. At the grand bus station in Vienna, Hungarians got free tickets to anywhere they wanted to go in Europe. Each bus was labeled with a different capital—take your choice: Paris, Rome, Bonn, Madrid, Amsterdam, Brussels, Lisbon and beyond—London, Stockholm, Copenhagen . . .

My mother's aunt from the Bronx, "the Tante," met us in Vienna and took us out to a radiant café for lunch, a café to rival any in Budapest (and that's saying a lot). She gave my parents a thousand American dollars to do with as we pleased. She then offered to set us up in New York. She told us that she and her husband owned three kosher butcher shops in the Bronx, and we would be well fed and well looked after in America. My father's first cousin from Toronto offered to set us up in Canada. He had escaped ten years before and had opened a successful radio shop. He let us know in a telegram that we could stay with him and his family until we found our footing. It was great to have the choice, but refugee agencies and western counties in general were generous with relocation subsidies and possibilities, and like us many had relatives who had preceded them to the free world.

That night my parents had a colossal argument. I'll never forget the screaming. Helpers in the army barracks shooed them outside. My grandmother hugged me and clamped my ears shut when she found me crying in my cot.

My father said he was not going to America to become a butcher. He had not been able to become a lawyer because of the anti-Jewish laws instituted in 1939 (when he turned eighteen). He'd become a tool and die maker and felt he could do better on his own in Canada. He badly wanted to make it on his own. He had been born into wealth, and it was all gone, so he had a chance to prove he could do it. But not as a butcher. My father's cousin said he could get him a job as a skilled worker at General Motors just outside Toronto.

My parents agreed to meet the Tante the next day and to flip a coin. Tails was Canada. Heads was the Bronx. Tails it was. So Canada it became.

What an astonishing fate awaited us in the New World, in Toronto. My father always said he'd brought us to a country "without issues," which of course wasn't true. For one, what had we Europeans done to the First Nations people we had pushed aside, then tried to "cleanse" of their "savagery"?

But what was true was that in the New World people from many countries, people like us, had to live together and had to make it work, had to do so in harmony. Heterogeneity seemed to be the key. As cultures in Europe and everywhere else, it seemed, remained homogeneous, they often viewed outsiders as Other, as different and therefore to be looked upon with suspicion. The other memorable thing my father used to say, after years in Canada, was that "Europe is a failed experiment. It should be paved over and turned into a parking lot."

So most of the dark events of my life occurred before I started school. Most of my history, too, was loaded with dark events. The darkness followed us to the New World where, if it didn't dissipate, certainly it faded.

It is a natural defensive impulse to worry that others might represent some kind of threat. The Otherness problem is a serious one because it implies division and is therefore—what else?—divisive.

Just by chance we came to a land that was struggling to find its identity. It had evolved away from Britain. It had not risen up against it the way America had. It had sidled up to the world's greatest power just to the south of us, a power that was to dominate culture and language and modern thinking for more than a century, spreading its character over the face of the planet, some people adoring it and some abhorring it in equal measure.

The Canada of my childhood was sandwiched between the UK and the United States, Janus-like, not knowing which way we were facing much of the time and not certain who we were, quite. In fact, if I can extend the metaphor, we were facing both ways at once and only rarely glancing straight ahead into the mirror.

If Chicago is the Second City, Canada is the Second Country. Rich, vast, free, broad-minded, tolerant, liberal, but Outside. We are outsiders. No Canadian Prime Minister would ever pronounce herself or himself to be the "leader of the free world," except in a comedy routine. We are good at comedy because we are ever the outsider, looking in on the earth-shaking power we have next door. Outsiders, ever-observant, are the best at comedy: Jews, Irish, blacks, homosexuals, minorities of all kinds.

And what a cool power the United States has been. For too long, I desperately wanted to be American. I majored in American Lit. I was stirred by the bold songs, especially "The Star-Spangled Banner," the bold spirit of independence. Just crossing the border from Ontario into New York thrilled me. It was the Great Magnet, which pulled all eyes toward it with such force that no one could look away. Billions of people watch the Oscars. Think of how significant that is. Think of how preposterous it is. It is because all eyes are on America. (Now more than ever.)

Quebec is almost the proof of what I'm saying. In Quebec, one of Canada's biggest provinces, people speak French. They have revolted against the dominance of English Canada for centuries, but it is not English Canada that has propagated English culture and language, nor even the old oppressor Britain. It has been America. Quebecers are Canadians. And if Canada is the Second Country, Quebecers feel as if they live in the Third Country. (Never mind Mexico. Who knows what place they think they occupy—or some Americans think Mexicans occupy—on this continent?)

And so we differ somewhat in the way we view refugees. It's the greatest thing about Canada, a thing we stumbled on quite by accident and that has become part of our nature.

Unlike America, refugees here searched for a national identity. The United States has been the proverbial melting pot. Canada is a salad. Some call it a mosaic. We retain our original identities somewhat. The hyphen is harder, more obdurate. I remain a Hungarian-Jewish-Canadian. (The hyphen might be hardening in America too, as populist sentiments darken against newcomers.)

Another remarkable difference is that, in my lifetime, Canada has moved from a pre-national state to a post-national state without ever stopping at national. We Canadians love Canada, but we are anti-nationalist at the same time. We didn't break away from Mother England in a revolution, as I said. We drifted away. We believe in "peace, order, and good government" more than "the pursuit of happiness," though the two aims are not mutually exclusive. Then there is Hungary, the place we left, still caught up in its vain nationalism to the exclusion of minorities. Nationalism is connected with ego and connected with intolerance because it again implies that others are "Other," people with different aspirations, different values.

The overwhelming majority of people fleeing oppressive regimes, like Syria, the way we did from the Soviets, want what we wanted: freedom, security, peace, quiet, shelter, food, decent work, education, a new language, a new way of seeing things, and hope, hope, hope. There are exceptions, of course: extremists and radical thinkers. But most—almost all—are not bursting to commit crimes. They want a future and are willing, for the most part, to relinquish their past, except for the richness it can add to the fabric of the New World, the new tapestry, illuminated and enriched by them. By us.

13 Ways of Being an Immigrant

POROCHISTA KHAKPOUR

I

The year is 1983 and Cabbage Patch Kids are at the height of popularity. You want one but you know your parents can't afford it. Just a couple years into this country and they keep saying they will go back to Iran soon—that the war will be over, that the revolution will be done, that you will be a refugee and alien no more. But for now, there is no money for things. At school, you know you are one of the few kids with less access to things and you know those others are not from here too. You work with them to get out of ESL and you try to act like kids who belong here, who have money. One way to do this is to have a Cabbage Patch Kid doll but this seems impossible. Still, your mother takes you to Toys"R"Us which seems like the greatest place on earth, second only to Disneyland which you've only heard about at this point, since it costs too much to go. At Toys"R"Us, several aisles are devoted to the Cabbage Patch dolls—if it were a farm, this area would be the Cabbage Patch. Their chubby faces peer at you from behind the plastic of their boxes. You have not considered which one you want because you don't think you will ever get one. Maybe an imitation at some point, one without a signature on the butt, which is how you've heard you know they are real; true Cabbage Patch Kids, the real ones, come with butt tattoos. You are looking at them longingly, when your mother points to a section down the aisle. There is a big sign: SALE. There is a whole section of Cabbage Patch Kids on sale, it turns out, and your mother is telling you they are in your budget, but she doesn't think they are the right ones for you. You are elated, then confused—why would she think that? And then you look at them, one by one, row after row. What do they have in common? They are black, all of them, the sale ones. You think about it. They could be your adopted child, why not. You are still too young to know how babies are made, so you don't think much deeper. You reach out to a pigtailed black one in a yellow track suit and you tell your mother that this is your daughter. Her name turns out to be Clover Stephanie and you still have her somewhere in storage. Her cheek is a bit scraped and looks white underneath. It bothers you, that fact. It bothers you also that you only have Clover because she was on sale, because she was black, but that was your first lesson about America, so maybe it was worth it.

II

You want to be a good student, the best in fact. One way to do this is to follow directions. In kindergarten, this is a big goal of yours, since English is still new. One rule is that at lunchtime, you must eat your dessert last. Dessert is usually a piece of fruit, but apparently it is hard for the kids to obey this rule. Not you. You always get it right. Your best friend is a blonde girl named Angela, who all the teachers love. She doesn't always play by the rules, but she gets away with it always. One day, she eats her cantaloupe before her spaghetti. This shocks you. You try to tell her to stop it, that she can't do this, but she does it. Without any fear, a smile even. You tell her to stop or you will have to tell on her. She smiles with a mouth full of cantaloupe. She is fearless. You tell her to stop right now, because you are truly about to tell. She laughs, more cantaloupe on her tongue. You can't take it anymore. You tell on her. The teaching assistant is a big man named Mr. Mondo and he is tough on the rules. He will take care of this. You walk right up to him and as much as it pains you, you point right at her. "Angela is eating her dessert first, Mr. Mondo." At this point, Angela is still, a look of fright on her face. She is not taunting you anymore. Good, you think, this might teach her. Mr. Mondo walks with you to her. He asks her if she did it. She nods, sadly. "Sorry," she says. He says nothing and pauses. Then he turns to you and he looks angry. He says one word: "Snitcher." He walks away and Angela smiles and you begin to cry and—after you learn what that word means, though from the start you know it's bad—once again you learn a lesson about America.

III

Your best friend in second grade lives in the good part of town. So does everyone at your elementary school. You got to that school because your zone was full. You live in the bad part of town. No one you know lives there too. Your dad drives a Pinto while your best friend's dad drives a Rolls-Royce. She hates it. You go to her house which is a mansion in the hills. She has so many expensive toys—numerous Cabbage Patch dolls, all white even though she is Vietnamese. She was born in America, unlike you. Her dad is a truck driver who also flips houses while yours is a professor. Another lesson, you one day realize.

IV

The usual substitute teacher, the one everyone in your grade sees most often, makes funny jokes and one is that he calls you "my Iranian sweetheart." You hate this, because you know Americans don't like Iran and you don't want to be singled out and teased—especially not because of being Iranian. But he always does this. Another teacher sticks his thumb in your mouth when he spots you sticking your tongue out at a friend. You don't know what it means, but it feels wrong. Years later, a science teacher offers you massages after class. You decline. A few grades down, a German teacher tells you you are so beautiful—he whispers it to you and you never come near him again. That same year, a librarian tells you about the male and female plugs too eagerly, demonstrating over and over. Another teacher laughs when students say you look like Anne Frank and makes a joke about him looking like a German soldier. You remember his bad breath on your face as he laughs at you, all over you. "Are there Jews still in Iran?" he asks you, but you don't answer. In America, adults are inappropriate, you realize, maybe a lesson for this place but maybe not.

V

You became editor-in-chief of your high school paper, your one and only dream in life. For two years, you have this post. You love nothing more. When your advisor is fired—a gay man, most likely fired for being gay in a homophobic school—you are incensed and you walk out and your staff follows. You are now seen as a rebel. This somehow seems very American. Your fearlessness also seems very American. You are blonde Angela with the cantaloupe. You must belong here if you think you can afford to leave.

VI

You go to college in New York—your dream—and you get your first internship at the *Village Voice*. You are a teenager and a scholarship kid and you have no money, and it does not occur to you that students ask their parents for money. You are left wondering how you can make this work so you learn to jump trains. Another scholarship kid teaches you. You get good at this—you go to your internship three times a week, and use some change for dinner: Pop-Tarts from the vending machine. And then you jump the train back. Part of it is you must look well-dressed to do this. You pretend you are dressing up for your internship. But you are doing it because they suspect you less if you look fancy. One time, you get caught. A female conductor. She tells you she's been watching you for months. You have no money to give her so she tells you your luck is up and she's kicking you out. It's midnight and the stop is Mount Vernon, a bad neighborhood. You are let out there and an old man offers you a drive home. You have no other choice. You stop jumping trains but you also stop internships altogether. They must not be for you.

VII

Sometimes you stay out all night. You miss the last train back to college upstate on purpose, knowing the next one is at 6 AM. No worries. The clubs are open all night. You go to them and lose yourself in them. In America, you fit in at clubs more than anywhere else. They are for you. It's there that people accept you the most. Very little matters in the forever night of a club and you learn then to forever trust darkness more than light.

VIII

You go on your year abroad to Oxford. You joke that you are doing it to dry out from drugs and drinking but it's somewhat true. There you find more clubs and more drugs and drinking. They call you "American Express," that group of boys you sleep with. You're just amazed they call you American.

IX

At age nineteen, you are raped. At age twenty, you are raped again. This strikes you as something that happens to American girls, a rite of passage. You tell no one, what American girls seem to do too or not do.

X

When 9/11 happens outside your East Village window, you remember your first nightmares as a recent immigrant in the eighties. It was always the same: men in dark clothing with machine guns and machetes loose on your city streets. They were terrorists and you were the hostages. In your dream, it's always in Iran. In your dream, you are safe in America. But not in reality, you realize, after 9/11. Your old world has now come for you. This is what being an American looks like now, you think, as you take your shoes off in an airport security line for the first time.

XI

You become a published author. An American author. No, an Iranian-American author. Never does the hyphen matter more than when you are an author, it seems.

XII

In your teens, you contemplate suicide. In your twenties, you contemplate suicide. In your thirties, you contemplate suicide. You are now about a hundred days from turning forty and you wonder how many more times you will contemplate suicide. You wonder if you'd been happier in that other life you were meant to live: the one where you stayed in Iran and maybe got married and had kids and maybe never became a writer. Maybe even you would have already died of suicide.

XIII

You are now sixteen years an American—you become an American in November 2001—and you realize you could have had a child in that time. You have no kids, no husband, no home you own, no roots in this country. No real reason to be here. Trump becomes president and your country is on the list of one of the six countries of the "Muslim ban." You are suddenly always a Muslim. Suddenly no one doubts your brownness anymore. You realize every day is a lesson in America, the real America, the violent one that never protected you. You remember blonde Angela with the cantaloupe glistening in her laughing mouth and you think for the first time she was maybe laughing at you. Why would you think you'd get anywhere here? On Facebook, you beg your white friends to do better, you ask them for ideas on where to live, you try to imagine another future they have. You wonder if your Americanness is forever and if you will die an American. You realize it might be just as hard to shake being an American as it was to become one in the first place. You realize with joy you will die an American; you realize with agony you will die an American; you realize with horror and confusion and fear and disbelief that you will die an American. Somehow it is harder to imagine than dying.

You wonder who has died because of your will to become an American, and you wonder also if they look like you.

Refugees and Exiles

MARINA LEWYCKA

When I used to read the stories of refugees, mothers and children being plucked from leaky boats off the coast of Turkey and Libya, or young people's bodies washed up lifeless on Mediterranean shores, it was all terribly sad, I thought, but nothing to do with me.

After all, I was comfortably settled in the UK, with a state pension, a lifetime as a British taxpayer behind me, and, most important of all, a British passport.

I had got my first British passport when I was twenty-two years old. Until then, I had traveled around Europe as a teenager on an "Alien's Travel Document," blue with two black stripes. My older sister, who was born in Ukraine, had a blue travel document with one black stripe, which meant that she was stateless. My two black stripes meant that my alien nationality was officially "undetermined"—I had been born in a German "displaced persons" camp after the end of World War II. So strictly speaking my family were not even refugees—we were forced laborers who sought refuge in the West rather than going back to Stalin's Soviet Union.

I have a photo of myself in that camp, in an old-fashioned pram with big curly springs. I was a very cute, plump baby, far from the malnourished, stick-thin, vacant-eyed babies we have come to associate with refugees. I don't know how my parents were able to afford such a splendid pram. Maybe some kind person had donated it. I have no memory of the camp, or of what it felt like to be that baby.

By the time they were in their early thirties, my parents, both born in 1911, had experienced the two world wars, two revolutions, a continuous civil war, two famines, Stalin's purges in which my grandfather was murdered, the terror of the British air raids on Kiel where I was born. No wonder that by the time they arrived in Sussex in 1948 all they wanted was a quiet life.

We arrived in England in 1947 or 1948 when I was about two, and we were taken in first of all by the Dobbses, a middle-class family of progressive views who lived in East Sussex. (Kitty Dobbs was a relative of Beatrice Webb, an activist in the democratic socialist Fabian Society founded in Britain in the nineteenth century.) Once in Britain, my parents worked hard, feared the law, and did their best to make themselves invisible. They didn't talk to me about the traumas they had lived through. They wanted to spare me all that suffering—but I picked it up anyway, from books with photographs, from eavesdropping on late-night conversations when they thought I was asleep. I grew up afraid of the past, and until I started to write my first novel when I was in my fifties, I didn't visit it much.

Around 1950 we moved to Yorkshire into our first home of our own, a two-up two-down terraced house in a mining village; all we had to endure was the ineluctable nosiness of our coal miner neighbors, diluted with countless cups of tea. People were kind to us, and very curious. And of course it helped that the Russians and Ukrainians had been allies of the British, and suffered massive losses, in what my parents still spoke of as the Great Patriotic War.

At school I was bullied by a gang of little boys—the same little boys who pulled the wings off butterflies, stamped on worms, and made life a misery for fat kids, kids who wore glasses, or those who were seen to be *swots* (as I was). In other words, then as always, there were bullies on the lookout for vulnerable victims.

I got my revenge by coming top in everything, and by being more English than the English. The stories I read as a child, like *Winnie the Pooh, Alice in Wonderland,* and *The Lion, the Witch, and the Wardrobe,* were the staples of a comfortable middle-class English childhood; I didn't seem to notice how very different the children in those stories were to my own migrant childhood. I read English literature at university, and spent my weekends cycling around Cotswold villages and rubbing brasses. I fell madly in love with English poetry and English wit and when I graduated I went on to be an English teacher. I blended in so totally that even I forgot that I wasn't *really* English.

So the rising volume of anti-immigrant anti-refugee rhetoric in the popular press in the twenty-first century took me quite by surprise—these didn't seem to me to be the same English people I had grown up amongst, who regularly arrived on our doorstep with a fresh-baked cake or an invitation to dinner. Did they really hate us so much?

The voices grew uglier and more clamorous. A former contestant on the reality show *The Apprentice* turned columnist called Katie Hopkins reaped a huge popular following by publicly calling refugees "cockroaches" and suggesting holes be drilled in their boats to help them sink. "Show me bodies floating in water," she wrote, and "skinny people looking sad. I still don't care."

Soon "economic migrant" rather than "refugee" became the accepted term for people fleeing wars and natural disasters (even ones which directly or indirectly had been caused by the West), suggesting that these people were merely trying to better themselves financially and were therefore undeserving of our help. "Bogus" became the epithet of choice for "asylum seeker," as though people were just *pretending* to flee from persecution. The *Daily Mail*, one of the newspapers which employed Katie Hopkins, and which had backed Oswald Mosley and the British Union of Fascists in the 1930s, led the clamor with increasingly lurid headlines about floods of refugees and migrants heading for the British Isles.

It became impossible to ignore those voices, impossible not to take sides. A young woman MP, Jo Cox, who was supportive of migrants, was murdered in the street by a far-right extremist during the EU referendum campaign. I found reading the *Daily Mail* was becoming increasingly upsetting, especially the readers' comments, which spewed misspelt torrents of hatred in all directions. In retrospect, I was not surprised to learn, later on, that less educated people and older people were more likely to hold anti-Europe views. Interestingly, I noticed that some of those hate-filled letters came from addresses registered in the United States but the British and U.S. rhetoric was the same.

It all came to a head in the UK with the EU referendum in June 2016, and with hindsight it is easy to see that much of this refugee-phobia was part of an orchestrated campaign to persuade ordinary Britons, many of whom had never knowingly seen a refugee except on television, to cast their vote for Brexit in the referendum. Places with the lowest number of migrants and refugees, like Wales and Cornwall, also recorded the highest anti-immigrant sentiment. Of course they probably *had* seen refugees—people like myself, not the huddled desperate dangerous characters who were portrayed in the popular media.

The vote to leave the EU seemed at that time, and it still seems, a monumental act of national self-destruction, driven largely by drummed-up foreigner-phobia including the entire population of Turkey, which was poised to migrate to the UK, we were told. At the same time, through some of the British media, we were hearing of a similar hate-filled drumbeat echoing from across the Atlantic. Katie Hopkins revealed herself as a big Trump fan, and vowed she would move to America if he won the U.S. election (but she's still here!). Would our sophisticated American cousins turn out to be as foolish and gullible as we had been? You bet.

At least, we believed, their folly was limited to eight years and could easily be reversed at four. Those who lived through the triumph of Trump would see an end to it in the not too distant future. Whereas I would live out my days in this strangely altered country—Brexit was for the whole of the rest of our lives, and our children's and grandchildren's.

Maybe what I did not appreciate, both in the United States and in the UK, was that the Trump strategy, like the Brexit strategy, was not intended to be limited in its scope or time frame. It was a deliberate attempt to shift the whole political conversation rightward. Things which had been off-limits before, ideas that could not be expressed, words which could not be used in polite company, were now freely and ubiquitously said in the public domain. A German friend of mine, who taught German in a local school, walked into his classroom the day after the referendum to find all the children frenziedly banging their desk lids and chanting "BREXIT! BREXIT!" Random acts of violence against "foreigners," always present at a low level, became commonplace and unremarkable. Women wearing burqas were assaulted on public transport. I witnessed someone rushing up to a complete stranger whom they deemed to be a foreigner in a busy street and shouting into her face, "We voted for you to go home! Now go!" My parents had sought refuge in one country—the tolerant and generous Britain of the NHS, the BBC, Oxfam, free cod-liver oil and orange juice for the young, free milk and meals in school, good wages ensured by strong trade unions, and Yorkshire neighborliness. I grew up with all the advantages of post-war prosperity underpinned by the post-war consensus, a strong welfare state, heritor to a rich centuries-old culture with the jewel of the cunning and subtle English language as my native tongue. It feels now as though I am destined to live out my days in a very different country—a Britain of austerity, private provision, short term contracts and the minimum wage, a crude and violent language in the popular press which urged the prime minister to wage war on the 48 percent of people who like me had opposed Brexit, calling on her to "crush the saboteurs!"

My daughter and her African partner have left Britain for good; my grandchildren will not be able to make themselves at home here. Like hundreds of foreigners who have settled here, I am marooned in this land which is my home and not my home, once a place of refuge, now reminding us that we are and always been have aliens.

In the event, the June 2017 election, which was supposed to deliver to our prime minister unprecedented powers, revealed a Britain which is bitterly divided between social classes and between generations, in which no one feels really at home. So where do I belong now, I wonder? In the rural shambolic Ukraine of my parents' memories—not even my own memories? In Germany where I was born, now rebuilt and prosperous, whose post-war decades of soul-searching have brought it face to face with the darkness and horror that can lie at the heart of a bid for "national greatness"? Or here among British people, who treated me with such kindness when I was a refugee, but never, it seems, saw me as one of them? Maybe as with all of us the country which is our true home is the idyllic rose-tinted land of our own childhood, from which we are always exiles.

This Is What the Journey Does

MAAZA MENGISTE

I watch the young man getting ready to cross a busy intersection from my table inside a café next to a large window. The orange glow of a late afternoon sun drapes him in thick sheets, lying across his shoulders and accenting his face. I recognize him for the East African that he is, a young man of Eritrean or Ethiopian origin with a slender frame, delicate features, and large eyes. He has the gaunt look of other recently arrived immigrants that I have met, a thinness that goes beyond a natural state of the body. He moves differently from one accustomed to the space he inhabits; his gait is a series of cautious, jagged steps forward. He appears frightened, overly sensitive to those who brush past him. He seems as if he is trying to coil inside himself, shrink enough to avoid being touched. Though I can note all of these details, I know there is nothing really special about him, not in Florence, Italy. He is just one of the many refugees or migrants who have made their way here from East Africa, a physical embodiment of those now-familiar reports and photographs of migration.

Pedestrians amble past on the narrow sidewalk, casting long shadows in the golden light of dusk. They are caught up in their private conversations, lost in the steady rhythm of their exchanges. They are unaware of the young man I am watching through the large window, brushing past my own reflection to get a better look. They do not realize that he is picking up speed behind them, his body stiffening with each passing second. He bends forward at the chest, slightly at first, then as if he might tip from his own momentum. He moves that way for several paces before he starts to push past pedestrians, oblivious to those he nearly trips. He is a wild, wayward figure careening carelessly through the busy sidewalk, distracted by his own thoughts.

Then, abruptly, he stops. He is so still that curious eyes turn on him, this sunlit figure stepping calming into the middle of the busy intersection. He stands there, immobile and slightly stunned as cars come to a halt and motorcyclists slow. Traffic waits for him to move. Instead, he begins to gesture, a conductor leading an invisible orchestra. His bony arms bend and extend, propelled by an energy only growing stronger. Each sweep of his hand pulls the rest of him upward then twists him in an awkward circle. He continues as observers pause, then shake their heads and walk on by. Soon, he is working his mouth around words, and even before he starts, I know he is about to shout.

I let everything else disappear so I can focus on the developing scene. People move past him, irritated but still polite. Motorists carefully angle around his intruding figure. Everyone ignores him as best as they can, treating him as no more than a mild disturbance, unremarkable. He continues gesticulating, his head turning one way then the other, his actions getting progressively faster. There is a strange kind of rhythm beginning, an erratic dance that is leaving him desperate to keep pace. While I watch, something squeezes against my chest and makes me take a sudden breath. I don't understand the ache that fills me. Or maybe I just do not want to recognize it. Maybe I do not want to find the words because to do so would mean to tumble down somewhere else, somewhere dark, far from this bright and busy street.

I have come to the café to escape the day's barrage of disturbing news. I have come with a notebook and my pen to distance myself from reminders of the turbulence continuing in America, in Ethiopia, in the Mediterranean, in the Middle East, in Europe: everywhere. I have come to find a way out of what I know in order to make my way toward a space where I can imagine, unhindered by unnecessary distractions. I have come to be alone, to write in solitude, free of the noise that has seemed to follow me for months, or perhaps it has been years. It is hard to know how to measure time, how to orient oneself when horror and shock begin to embed themselves into the pulse of daily life. It has become easy to live in the present moment, to spin from one disturbing event to the next, to move so quickly between disasters that entire days are spent in stupefied surprise.

Lazarus, I think, as I keep watching this young man: A defiant body refusing stillness, resisting quietness. A body using noise to stay alive, to move, to be seen. The waitress comes to take my order and smiles down at my notebook. I notice the couple next to me eyeing it warily, as if they are afraid I am taking notes on their conversation. No one seems to be aware of the drama unfolding outside the café where a young black man with unkempt hair is spinning in increasingly wide circles, motioning wildly, shouting incoherently at passersby. He is a spectacle without an audience. He is an actor in Shakespeare's tale, full of sound and fury.

He spins and flings his arms. He throws up a hand and snaps his wrist. He closes a palm over an ear and listens to his own whispers. He frowns and smiles, laughs alone, then twirls and catches another stranger's stare. There is anger in his spastic energy. There is sorrow and confusion in his eyes. He is breaking, I say to myself, and doing what he can to keep himself together. My reflection catches my eye and so I put my head down and in my notebook I write: "You did not leave home like this. This is what the journey does." It comes again, that ache in the middle of my chest. For a moment, it is so strong that I am sure he can feel it. I am certain it is a tether binding us together and he will turn in just the right way and I will be exposed. If he looks at me, then our lives will unfold and in front of us will be the many roads we have taken to get to this intersection in Florence and we will reveal ourselves for what we are: immigrant, migrant, refugee, African, East African, black, foreigner, stranger, a body rendered disobedient by the very nature of what we are.

When I glance up again, the young man has quieted down. Now, he looks almost bored as he weaves between pedestrians while twisting a lock of hair around a skinny finger. He moves lazily, as if he has accomplished what he set out to do. From where I sit, it looks like he is walking toward me but he is simply following the sidewalk, and soon it will force him to proceed directly past the open door of the café where I am. As he saunters past, I notice a small bald patch on the back of his head. It is a perfect circle, as if a round object was placed on his scalp to burn away his hair through to his skin. I tell myself that I cannot possibly know what it is, that it could be an illusion, it could be just a leaf stuck in his hair, but that is not enough to keep myself from flinching.

Stories come back to me, told by a friend who crossed the Sahara to get to Europe by way of North Africa. He spoke of horrifying treatment at the hands of human traffickers and police in detention centers and makeshift prisons. He shared what he could and skipped the rest. In moments when several who made the journey were gathered, I would watch them point to their scars to help fill the lapses in their stories. Sometimes, there was no language capable of adding coherence to what felt impossible to comprehend. Sometimes, it was only the body that bore the evidence, pockmarks and gashes forming their own vocabulary. Staring at the busy intersection, I don't want to consider what this young man might have gone through to arrive in Italy, to be in the street on this day. That he is alive is a testament to his endurance. What he has been subjected to, what might have caused that scar, what was too much for his mind to balance—these thoughts lead the way to far darker realities than I can possibly know. I look back at the first note I took upon seeing him: "You did not leave home like this. This is what the journey does."

Lazarus was gifted the chance to walk again in the land of the living. On one hand, it was a simple proposition: He obeyed the command to stand up and he was able to live. The rest of his days pale in the brilliant light of this astounding miracle. It is easy to imagine that he moved gracefully through his new existence, a man pulsing with this exposure to divine grace and might. We want to think that when he rose from the dead, he did so untainted and unburdened. That it was a rebirth, free of unsettling wisdom. But Lazarus was an ordinary man who opened his eyes to find himself incomprehensible. Somewhere between the end of this life and his second chance, he shifted forms, became a miracle and a stranger, remolded from loved one to aberration.

Medical science understands death to be a process rather than a single event. Though it might feel cataclysmic and sudden, the body undergoes several functions before it no longer lives. The various organs that support it collapse one by one. They all must cease all activity for an extended period of time in order for a person to be declared dead. It is not sufficient for the heartbeat and circulation alone to stop, for example, they must cease long enough for the brain to also die. The end of life involves a journey, a series of steps before that ultimate destination. A body requires certain signposts to nudge it in the right direction. An abrupt shift in that progressive movement disrupts the order of things. It deforms a natural process and leaves behind something warped and unrecognizable.

Perhaps this explains Lazarus's complete silence in John 11 and 12 in the Bible. To give him a voice would mean to grapple with the messiness that his resurrection created. It would be to insert a complex, human component to a direct and potent lesson. Though the Sanhedrin wanted to kill him along with Jesus Christ, though his resurrected life and all that it represented was as much a threat to them as the claims of Jesus, he is not allowed to speak. Lazarus is a muted miracle, still alive today as a metaphor for uncanny second chances. We have found many ways to make use of his example but we do not know what to do with the living man. In part, it is because the Bible reveals so little about him. His story ends when he is no longer convenient. But to assume that he became worthless once he stepped free from his grave is to shrink his life down to its most significant moment. It is to believe that nothing else can possibly matter after so great a feat. It is to embrace the idea that we are, all of us, simple beings relentlessly pivoting around the same occurrence, trapped by the enormity of an important event, as if it is both the sun that guides us and the darkness that leaves us spinning in uncertain space.

There is a phrase found in medieval Chinese literature to explain the biological phenomenon of an ailing body that revives, suddenly and briefly, only to collapse and die. It is *hui guang fan zhao*, translated as "last glow before sunset," that brief shimmer before night. I think of this as the café where I sit begins to empty and a new set of patrons streams in. A DJ near me starts to spin his music against the slowly darkening sky outside. Through the window at my side, I gaze past my own reflection to focus on the unbroken flow of pedestrians and motorists at the intersection. The young man I observed earlier is gone, and in his place, routine and repetition have stepped in. I see him for a moment, though, leaving home, wherever that might have been, and making the tortuous trek through the Sahara. I see him trapped in containers and overloaded trucks and crowded boats. I see him struggle with a deadening stillness, then step onto land to face the boundaries set up in Europe. The journey is designed to test the body's resilience. Its intent is to break a human being and rearrange them inside. Every inch forward is a reminder of one's frailty. You do not arrive the same as when you left. You will sometimes look at a stranger and recognize yourself reflected in that new life: impossibly alive, walking through the lingering glow of a splendid sun while trying to spin free of a permanent darkness.

The Ungrateful Refugee

DINA NAYERI

I

A few weeks ago I dusted off my expired Iranian passport photo, an unsmiling eight-year-old version of me—stunned, angry, wearing tight gray hijab and staring far beyond the camera. It's not the face of a child on the verge of rescue, though I would soon escape Iran. I have kept that old photograph hidden since the day I threw away my last headscarf, and now it's the bewildered face and parted lips, not the scarf, that capture my interest. No matter how hard I try, I can't reconcile this child with the frazzled American writer in my recent pictures.

In 1985, when I was six years old, my family left our home in Isfahan for several months to live in London. The move was temporary, a half-hearted stab at emigration; nonetheless, I was enrolled in school. In Iran I had only attended nursery, never school, and I spoke only Farsi.

At first, the children were welcoming, teaching me English words using toys and pictures, but within days the atmosphere around me had changed. Years later, I figured that this must have been how long it took them to tell their parents about the Iranian kid. After that, a group of boys met me in the yard each morning and, pretending to play, pummeled me in the stomach. They followed me in the playground and shouted gibberish, laughing at my dumbfounded looks. A few weeks later, two older boys pushed my hand into a doorjamb and slammed it shut on my little finger, severing it at the first segment. I was rushed to the hospital, carrying a piece of my finger in a paper napkin. The segment was successfully reattached.

I never went back to that school, but later, in the chatter of the grown-ups from my grandmother's church and even in my parents' soothing whispers, I heard a steady refrain about gratefulness. God had protected me and so I shouldn't look at the event in a negative light. It was my moment to shine! Besides, who could tell what had motivated those boys? Maybe they were just playing, trying to include me though I didn't speak a word of their language. Wasn't that a good thing?

Eventually we returned to Iran. I was put under a headscarf and sent to an Islamic girls' school.

Three years later, my mother, brother, and I left Iran for real, this time after my mother had been dragged to jail for converting to Christianity, after the moral police had interrogated her three times and threatened her with execution. We became asylum seekers, spending two years in refugee hostels in Dubai and Rome. By that time I had lived my first eight years in the belly of wartime Iran—for most of the 1980s, the Iran-Iraq war wrecked our country and trapped us in a state of almost constant fear. I had grown accustomed to the bomb sirens, the panicked dashes down to the basement, the taped-up windows. So the time that followed, the years in refugee hostels, felt peaceful, a reprieve from all the noise. My mother urged me to thank God in my prayers.

When I was ten, we were accepted by the United States and sent to Oklahoma, just as the first Gulf War began. By the time of our arrival in America, the nail on my pinkie had grown back, my hair was long, and I was (according to my mother) pretty and funny and smart. The first thing I heard from my classmates, however, was a strange "ching-chong"ese intended to mock my accent. I remember being confused, not at their cruelty, but at their choice of insult. A dash of racism I had expected—but I wasn't Chinese; were these children wholly ignorant to the shape of the world outside America? If you want to mock me, I wanted to say, dig down to the guttural *kh*s and *gh*s, produce some phlegm, make a camel joke; don't "ching-chong" at me, you mouth-breather. (See? I had learned their native insults well enough.)

Of course, I didn't say that. And I didn't respond when they started in on the cat-eating and the foot-binding. I took these stories home and my mother and I laughed over chickpea cookies and cardamom tea—fragrant foods they might have mocked if only they knew. By then it was clear to me that these kids had met one foreigner before, and that unfortunate person hailed from southeast Asia.

I needn't have worried, though; the geographically correct jokes were coming. Like the boys in London, these kids soon spoke to their parents, and within weeks, they had their "turban jockeys" and their "camel-fuckers" loaded and ready to go. Meanwhile, I was battling with my teacher over a papier-mâché topographical map of the United States, a frustrating task that was strangely central to her concerns about my American assimilation. When I tried to explain to her that only a few months before I had lived with refugees outside Rome, and that most of the social studies work baffled me, she looked at me sleepily and said: "Awww, sweetie, you must be so grateful to be here."

Grateful. There was that word again. Here I began to notice the pattern. This word had already come up a lot in my childhood, but in her mouth it lost its goodness. It hinted and threatened. Afraid for my future, I decided that everyone was right: if I failed to stir up in myself enough gratefulness, or if I failed to properly display it, I would lose all that I had gained, this Western freedom, the promise of secular schools and uncensored books.

The children were merciless in their teasing, and soon I developed a tic in my neck. Other odd behaviors followed. Each time something bad happened, I would repeat a private mantra, the formula I believed was the reason for my luck so far, and my ticket to a second escape—maybe even a life I would actually enjoy. I said it again and again in my head, and sometimes accidentally aloud:

I'm lucky. I'm grateful. I'm the smartest in my class.

I'm lucky. I'm grateful. I'm the smartest in my class.

That last sentiment (which I did a poor job of hiding) didn't go over too well. What right did I, a silly Iranian, have to think I was better than anyone?

Still, my mother suffered more. In Iran, she had been a doctor. Now she worked in a pharmaceuticals factory, where her bosses and coworkers daily questioned her intelligence, though they had a quarter of her education. The accent was enough. If she took too long to articulate a thought, they stopped listening and wrote her off as unintelligent. They sped up their speech and, when she asked them to slow down, they sighed and rolled their eyes. If someone messed up a formula, she was the sole target for blame.

The hate did eventually wane; some would say that that's the natural cycle of things. We assimilated. No longer dark strangers from war-torn lands, at some point we stopped frightening them. We went to work, to school, to church. We grew familiar, safe, no longer the outsiders.

I don't believe in that explanation. What actually happened was that we learned what they wanted, the hidden switch to make them stop simmering. After all, these Americans had never thought we were terrorists or Islamic fundamentalists or violent criminals. From the start, they knew we were a Christian family that had escaped those very horrors. And they, as a Protestant community, had accepted us, rescued us. But there were unspoken conditions to our acceptance, and that was the secret we were meant to glean on our own: we had to be grateful. The hate wasn't about being darker, or from elsewhere. It was about being those things and daring to be unaware of it. As refugees, we owed them our previous identity. We had to lay it at their door like an offering, and gleefully deny it to earn our place in this new country. There would be no straddling. No third culture here.

That was the key to being embraced by the population of our town, a community that openly took credit for the fact that we were still alive, but wanted to know nothing of our past. Month after month, my mother was asked to give her testimony in churches and women's groups, at schools and even at dinners. I remember sensing the moment when all conversation would stop and she would be asked to repeat our escape story. The problem, of course, was that they wanted our salvation story as a talisman, no more. No one ever asked what our house in Iran looked like, what fruits we grew in our yard, what books we read, what music we loved, and what it felt like now not to understand any of the songs on the radio. No one asked if we missed our cousins or grandparents or best friends. No one asked what we did in summers or if we had any photos of the Caspian Sea. "Men treat women horribly there, don't they?" the women would ask. Somehow it didn't feel OK to tell them about my funny dad with his pockets full of sour cherries, or my grandpa who removed his false teeth when he told ghost stories.

Such memories, of course, would imply the unthinkable: that Iran was as beautiful, as fun, as energizing and romantic, as Oklahoma or Montana or New York.

II

From then on, we sensed the ongoing expectation that we would shed our old skin, give up our former identities—every quirk and desire that made us us—and that we would imply at every opportunity that America was better, that we were so lucky, so humbled to be here. My mother continued giving testimonials in churches. She wore her cross with as much spirit as she had done in Islamic Iran. She baked American cakes and replaced the rosewater in her pastries with vanilla. I did much worse: over years, I let myself believe it. I lost my accent. I lost my hobbies and memories. I forgot my childhood songs.

In 1994, when I was fifteen, we became American citizens. I was relieved, overjoyed, and genuinely grateful. We attended a citizenship ceremony on the football field of a local college campus. It was the Fourth of July and dozens of other new citizens would be sworn in with us. It was a bittersweet day, the stadium filled with cheering locals, a line of men, women, and children winding around and around the field toward a microphone at the end zone, where each of us would be named and sworn in. I remember staring in wonder at the others in line: I didn't realize there were this many other brown and yellow people in

Oklahoma. Yes, there were a handful of black people, a few Jews here or there. But this many Indians? This many Sri Lankans and Pakistanis and Chinese and Bangladeshis and Iranians and Afghans? Where had they been hiding? (Not that I had looked.)

Halfway through the ceremony, an Indian man, around eighty years old, was led to the microphone, where he introduced himself and swore allegiance to the United States. When he was finished, he raised his fists and thrashed the sky. "I AM AMERICAN!" he shouted into the microphone. "FINALLY, I AM AMERICAN!" The crowd erupted, joining his celebration. As he stepped away, he wobbled and collapsed from the effort, but someone caught him. He turned back and smiled to the crowd to show he was OK, that this fit of joy hadn't killed him, then walked away.

That's my favorite day as an American, my first one, still unsurpassed. No one was putting on a face that day. No one felt obliged or humbled, imagining their truer home. That old man was heaving with love. The people in the stands were roaring with it. It's a complicated memory for me now. I refuse to deny the simple and vast beauty of it, though I know they cheered not the old man himself, but his spasm of gratitude, an avowal of transformation into someone new, into them.

Years passed. I became as American as a girl can be, moved far away, grew into my mind and body and surrounded myself with progressive, educated friends. The bad feelings disappeared. I started to love the Western world and thought of myself a necessary part of it. I moved around with ease, safely flashing my American passport, smiling brightly when customs officers squinted at my place of birth. It didn't matter: I was no longer an asylum seeker. I had long ago been accepted. I had a stellar education. My confidence showed (and maybe it helped that I had caramel highlights in my hair). Again and again I was welcomed "home" at JFK with a polite nod or a smile.

Other immigrants have written about this moment: the "welcome home" at JFK, its power on the psyche after long flights. For me, as soon as those words leave the officer's mouth, my confidence is replaced by a gush of gratitude. "Thank you!" I say breathlessly. Thank you for saying it's my home. Thank you for letting me in again. In that instant before my passport is returned to me, I'm the old man punching the air.

III

When I was thirty, I had another citizenship ceremony. This one wasn't the sleepless obsession that the American one had been. It was simply that I had married a French citizen, he had applied on my behalf, and, having passed the language and culture tests by a whisker, I became a Frenchwoman of sorts. I traveled a lot in those days and so I decided to have my fingerprints taken (the last step in the paperwork) on a stopover in New York. The police officer whose job it was to oversee the process asked why a nice girl like me needed fingerprints. I told him, to which he replied: "Couldn't you find an American man?"

Though I hadn't given it much thought back then, I said: "American men don't like me." He gave me a puzzled look, so I added, "The American men I know never try to impress you . . . or not me, at least. They think I should feel lucky to have them."

He gave a weary sigh. "No man likes to work for it."

"Some men work for it," I said, trying to sound defiant.

He laughed and bashed my fingers into the ink.

My second citizenship ceremony was held at the French

embassy in Amsterdam (my then home) beside families from Lebanon, Turkey, Tunisia, Morocco, and a number of sub-Saharan countries. The image that stays with me is of families singing the French national anthem, "La Marseillaise." The awe in their faces as they sang that song, every word practiced, moved me. Even the small children straightened their shoulders and sang from memory. I had made a stab at memorizing the words, but mostly I read off a sheet. I was proud, but they were experiencing something else: a transformation, a rebirth. They were singing their way into a joyous new life. I took a moment to think of that old Indian man from years before, to do an imaginary fist-pump in his honor.

I've been moving back and forth between New York and Europe pretty much my entire adult life. When I lived in Amsterdam, even highly educated people openly complained of "too many Moroccans and Turks" in certain neighborhoods. Geert Wilders, the head of the far-right Party for Freedom, had warned that the country would soon become "Nether-Arabia."

In Amsterdam, I got to know Iranian refugees who didn't have my kind of luck with their asylum applications. One man in our community set himself on fire in Dam Square in 2011. He had lived in Amsterdam for a decade, following their rules, filling out their papers, learning their culture, his head always down. He did all that was asked of him and, in the end, he was driven to erase his own face, his skin.

Remembering Kambiz Roustayi, a man who only wanted a visa, his family, and his own corner of the world, I want to lash out at every comfortable native who thinks that his kind don't do enough. You don't know what grateful is, I want to say. You haven't seen a young man burn up from despair, or an old man faint on a football field from relief and joy, or a nine-year-old boy sing the entire "Marseillaise" from memory. You don't know how much life has already been spent settling into the cracks of your walls. Sometimes all that's left of value in an exile's life is his identity. Please stop asking people to rub out their face as tribute.

IV

With the rise of nativist sentiment in Europe and America, I've seen a troubling change in the way people make the case for refugees. Even those on the left talk about how immigrants make America great. They point to photographs of happy refugees turned good citizens, listing their contributions, as if that is the price of existing in the same country, on the same earth. Friends often use me as an example. They say in posts or conversations: "Look at Dina. She lived as a refugee and look how much stuff she's done." As if that's proof that letting in refugees has a good, healthy return on investment.

But isn't glorifying the refugees who thrive according to Western standards just another way to endorse this same gratitude politics? Isn't it akin to holding up the most acquiescent as examples of what a refugee should be, instead of offering each person the same options that are granted to the native-born citizen? Is the life of the happy mediocrity a privilege reserved for those who never stray from home?

This semester, I'm teaching an American literature course at a private international school in London. My students have come with their families from all over the world and have empathy and insight, but for the most part, they have lived privileged lives. For the last semester, I've forced them to read nothing but "outsider fiction". Stories by immigrants and people of color.

Stories about poverty. Stories about being made to sit on the periphery. Most are loving it, but some are frustrated. "I've already learned the race stuff," one said, after our third story with a protagonist of color. More than one parent advised me that Bharati Mukherjee and James Baldwin are not important when these kids have yet to read "classic writers" such as Harper Lee (because how could they develop their literary taste if they hadn't first grounded themselves in the point of view of the impossibly saintly white family?).

Even among empathetic, worldly students, I'm finding a grain of this same kind of expectation: the refugee must make good. If, in one of our stories, an immigrant kills himself (Bernard Malamud's "The Refugee"), they say that he wasted his opportunity, that another displaced person would have given anything for a shot at America. They're right about that, but does that mean that Malamud's refugee isn't entitled to his private tragedies? Is he not entitled to crave death? Must he first pay off his debt to his hosts and to the universe?

Despite a lifetime spent striving to fulfill my own potential, of trying to prove that the West is better for having known me, I cannot accept this way of thinking, this separation of the worthy exile from the unworthy. Civilized people don't ask for resumes when answering calls from the edge of a grave. It shouldn't matter what I did after I cleaned myself off and threw away the last of my asylum-seeking clothes. My accomplishments should belong only to me. There should be no question of earning my place, of showing that I was a good bet. My family and I were once humans in danger, and we knocked on the doors of every embassy we came across: the UK, America, Australia, Italy. America answered and so, decades later, I still feel a need to bow down to airport immigration officers simply for saying "Welcome home."

But what America did was a basic human obligation. It is the obligation of every person born in a safer room to open the door when someone in danger knocks. It is your duty to answer us, even if we don't give you sugary success stories. Even if we remain a bunch of ordinary Iranians, sometimes bitter or confused. Even if the country gets overcrowded and you have to give up your luxuries, and we set up ugly little lives around the corner, marring your view. If we need a lot of help and local services, if your taxes rise and your street begins to look and feel strange and everything smells like turmeric and tamarind paste, and your favorite shop is replaced by a halal butcher, your schoolyard chatter becoming ching-chongese and phlegmy *kh*s and *gh*s, and even if, after all that, we don't spend the rest of our days in grateful ecstasy, atoning for our need.

In 2015, I moved to England again, a place I no longer associated with the permanently numb tip of my little finger, or the strange half-sensation of typing the letter "a" on a keyboard. I became a mother in a London hospital. Now I have a little girl who already looks Iranian. The first major event of her life was Brexit. The second was Trump's election. At 5 AM on Brexit morning, as I was feeding her, the memory of my pinkie returned. We had just learned of the referendum results. On Facebook, every former immigrant I knew released a collective shudder—all of them recalling their first days in England or America or Holland. They began sharing their stories. What I remembered was that boy who pushed my finger into the hinge of a door. That other boy who slammed the door shut. They're adults now. Most likely, they've lived lives much like their parents, the ones who taught them to hate me in 1985. Most likely they believe the same things. England doesn't want us, I thought. It doesn't want my daughter. It doesn't want me.

Nowadays, I often look at the white line through my pinkie nail, and I think I finally understand why gratefulness matters so much. The people who clarified it for me were my students, with their fresh eyes and stunning expectations, their harsh, idealistic standards that every person should strive and prove their worth, their eagerness to make sense of the world. They saw right through to the heart of the uneasy native.

During our discussion of Flannery O'Connor's "A Displaced Person," the class began unpacking Mrs. Shortley's hatred of Mr. Guizac, the Polish refugee whose obvious talents on the farm would soon lead to her mediocre husband's dismissal as a farmhand. "She's seen the images from the Holocaust, the piles of bodies in Europe," said one student. "So if one of those bodies in the pile can escape death and come to America and upend her life, then how much is she worth?"

I was stunned silent (a rare thing for me). By the time I formulated my next question the conversation had moved on, and so I presented the question to my next class. "Would anything be any different, then, if Mr. Guizac had been grateful to Mrs. Shortley for making room for him?"

Around the table every head shook. No. Of course not. Nothing would change. "Mrs. Shortley wants to be above him, to be benevolent, to have control," said one insightful student. "Once the guy starts doing better on his own, control goes, no matter how grateful he acts."

The refugee has to be less capable than the native, needier; he must stay in his place. That's the only way gratitude will be accepted. Once he escapes control, he confirms his identity as the devil. All day I wondered, has this been true in my own experience? If so, then why all the reverence for the refugees who succeed against the odds, the heartwarming success stories? And that's precisely it—one can go around in this circle forever, because it contains no internal logic. You're not enough until you're too much. You're lazy until you're a greedy interloper.

In many of the classes I've taught, my quietest kids have been Middle Eastern. I'm always surprised by this, since the literature I choose should resonate most with them, since I'm an Iranian teacher, their ally, since the civilized world yearns for their voices now. Still, they bristle at headlines about the refugee crisis that I flash on the screen, hang their heads, and look relieved when the class is finished. Their silence makes me angry, but I understand why they don't want to commit to any point of view. Who knows what their universe looks like outside my classroom, what sentiments they're expected to display in order to be on the inside.

Still, I want to show those kids whose very limbs apologize for the space they occupy, and my own daughter, who has yet to feel any shame or remorse, that a grateful face isn't the one they should assume at times like these. Instead they should tune their voices and polish their stories, because the world is duller without them—even more so if they arrived as refugees. Because a person's life is never a bad investment, and so there are no creditors at the door, no debt to repay. Now there's just the rest of life, the stories left to create, all the messy, greedy, ordinary days that are theirs to squander.

Am I a Refugee?

RAJA SHEHADEH

There are multiple times when I can interrogate my history to ask whether or not I'm a refugee.

I choose to start with my maternal grandfather, Salim Shehadeh. In the early years of the twentieth century he left Ramallah where he was born and travelled to the United States for education. Unlike many other Palestinians, he did not remain. After graduating with a doctorate from Cornell University and being naturalized as a US citizen, he returned to Palestine, then under British Mandate rule. He married and established his home in the coastal city of Jaffa, where he worked as a judge.

It was in Jaffa where my father, also originally from Ramallah, started his law office and married my mother. It was where their first born, my eldest sister, Siham, was born. They continued living there until attacks by Jewish forces on their city forced them to leave. My parents left by the end of April 1948 because they feared for their own safety and the well-being of their three-year-old daughter. They were among the 750,000 refugees who either fled or were forced out of their homes in those parts of Palestine that became Israel. The British police who were responsible for law and order and had voted for the 1947 United Nations Partition Plan did not carry out their responsibility of protecting the civilian Palestinian population of the country under their rule.

My parents had a summer house in the resort city of Ramallah where they escaped in the summer months from the oppressive heat and humidity of Jaffa. It was to this house they came to live, believing that their stay there would not exceed a few weeks. This was why they brought no winter clothing with them. That winter of 1948–49 proved one of the most severe in the region and they suffered the lack of warm clothing and harsh conditions living in a house not designed for the bitingly cold winter weather of Ramallah. As I was growing up I never experienced the hardship of the other Palestinian refugees who lived in camps. At least my family had a roof over their head.

I understood how convinced my father was that his return to Jaffa would be possible when looking through his papers after his death. There I found his optimistic reply to a letter from the man he appointed to take care of his house during their absence in 1948; my father assures the caretaker of their imminent return.

This conviction was not without basis. My father calculated that because Jaffa was in the Arab section, according to the United Nations Partition Scheme of 1947, the worst that could happen is that the Palestinians would lose part of their historic land, but Jaffa would remain theirs. Soon after they left Jaffa, he and many others who took refuge in Ramallah saw that the road back to their city remained open. And so along with colleagues he called for a meeting which was held at Cinema Dunia in Ramallah. There my father stood on the small stage in front of the screen and declared to those in attendance that tomorrow we will ride the cars and buses we used to travel to Ramallah and return back to our homes in Jaffa. There was huge excited applause and after the time and place where they were going to gather for the return trip was decided, they all left the successful convention. That night he and the other leaders were arrested by the Jordanian army in control of Ramallah and prevented from carrying out their planned return.

This incident has not been recorded in history books and few know about it. Cinema Dunia continued to stand in Ramallah until five years ago when it was demolished and an ugly shopping mall was built in its place. No sign has been placed commemorating this important and telling event.

Meanwhile the homes my parents and their fellow city-dwellers had left were used to accommodate Jewish refugees coming to the new state. There were a few cases when the newcomers refused to be given homes that belonged to others. The mother of the Israeli artists Dvora Morag, an Auschwitz survivor, was one of them. She said: "We cannot take the apartment in Jaffa, because we can't do what they did to us." But this was an exceptional case.

After the return proved impossible, my father refused to take a refugee card from the United Nations Relief and Works Agency (UNRWA). He didn't want handouts and was determined to fend for himself. UNRWA was set up in 1949 and now has some 4.9 million Palestinian refugees under its mandate. Palestinian refugees were specifically and deliberately excluded from the international refugee law regime established in 1951. Israel did not recognize those whom it had forced out of their homes in 1948 as refugees, nor did it acknowledge their right to return home. Instead it called them absentees. After 1948, those who tried to return to their homes Israel called infiltrators. Many were shot dead in the process.

For the first sixteen years of my life, I only heard about my parents' comfortable life in Jaffa and I felt deprived. I grew in Jordan, suffering difficult conditions in the same house my family had fled to after being forced out of the coastal city. But I never felt Jordanian. Then and always I've never been doubtful of my identity as a Palestinian.

Yet the country I felt I belonged to did not exist. The country was divided between the state of Israel that emerged in 1948 and Jordan which in 1950 annexed the West Bank. The Gaza Strip, another part of Palestine, was placed under Egyptian administration until its occupation by Israel in 1967.

This partition of Palestine lasted until 1967, when Israel occupied the West Bank, East Jerusalem, and the Gaza Strip. My father thought the time had come to end the conflict by creating a Palestinian state in the West Bank, East Jerusalem, and Gaza to live in peace alongside Israel. But Israel was not interested. What it wanted was to incorporate the occupied land of the West Bank and East Jerusalem into Greater Israel. A few weeks after the beginning of the occupation, East Jerusalem was annexed outright to Israel. The Gaza Strip was and continues to be tortured by being placed under a stifling siege. Over the past fifty-one years Israel has been annexing the West Bank piecemeal through the establishment of Jewish settlements that are to all intents and purposes considered part of Israel.

After the occupation of 1967 we were able to travel to Jaffa and see the home my parents left behind which had remained standing. It would have been possible then to end the conflict and start peace negotiations but with the hubris Israeli leaders felt after their victory in the 1967 war, they were in no mood to compromise. Yet this was not only a sign of the time. There is another more fundamental and persisting reason why peace remains elusive.

For Israel to recognize the *Nakba* (the catastrophe of 1948) would require an almost complete reshuffling of the country's foundation myth, which attempts to connect the land with the Jewish people bypassing any recognition of Palestinian presence there. The case of the village of Sataf, in the district of Jerusalem, provides a good demonstration of this process. It was one of some 400 Palestinian villages that were destroyed by Israel in the course of and after the 1948 war. In 1948 the village had a population of over 600. Due to limited availability of water, an extensive irrigation system was developed, and Sataf's agricultural produce was renowned locally. Three months after the establishment of the State of Israel, with no recorded resistance by the village inhabitants, they were forced out of their village and ended up in refugee camps in the West Bank. The village buildings were largely destroyed. Their lands became part of the Moshe Dayan Pine Forest while part of the remaining Palestinian village, with its terraces and irrigation system planned to save water, has been preserved by the Jewish National Fund as a historical theme park. The JNF website makes no mention of the Palestinian presence there; instead it speaks about demonstrating ancient Jewish agricultural and biblical farming techniques.

In his blog *Promised Land*, the Israeli blogger Noam Sheizaf recounts a childhood memory. On a school trip walking through excavations and listening to explanations from a tour guide about their ancestors who lived there two thousand years ago, one of the kids points to some ruins between the trees and asks: "Are these ancient homes as well?" His teacher answers: "These are not important."

What distinguishes the Palestinian case is not the loss of homes and property. There are many other cases in recent history of large groups of people forced to leave their homes. There was an exchange of population that involved hundreds of thousands of Greeks and Turks after the First World War. And in 1948, when India and Pakistan achieved independence, there was a massive exchange of populations, leaving some one million dead from communal violence. What distinguishes Palestine is that the loss was not of mere homes and properties but of an entire country.

In all these cases, however distressing their experience, the refugees had a place they could take refuge in, a remaining segment of their country to which they could come to belong. Not so in the case of the Palestinians. Their loss was entire. Even for those who managed to remain in the parts of Palestine that became Israel and who were granted Israeli citizenship, their status as second-class citizens was confirmed when Israel passed the Basic Law on July 19, 2018: Israel as the nation-state of the Jewish people. For them as for us, the consequences of the denial of what took place during the *Nakba* persists along with the refusal to recognize that Palestine and the Palestinian people ever existed.

Israel claims that when Palestinians insist on the recognition of their right of return, they are in effect asking for the state's destruction. In this, Israelis fail to realize that their freedom and the long-term survival of their country are only possible if the Palestinians have freedom and the two nations succeed in living together in peace and a recognition of the past. Until this happens I, who still live in Ramallah in a small and fragmented area of occupied Palestine, continue to be a refugee.

A Refugee Again

VU TRAN

When I was younger, I never thought of myself as a refugee. In my mind, I was an immigrant. A Vietnamese-American. A permanent foreigner with U.S. citizenship. A *refugee* felt like a thing of the past, a provisional status I once held that suggested vulnerability, inferiority, alienness—everything I wanted to remove from my idea of myself.

I arrived in America at the age of five, too young to appreciate my own perilous journey here. I quickly forgot the six days my mother and sister and I spent at sea, on a fishing boat with ninety people. I quickly forgot the deserted Malaysian island where we lived for four months, in a refugee camp of thousands. And then there was my first time on a plane, headed for Oklahoma, and my first time meeting my father, five years after he was forced to flee Vietnam without us. I only recently remembered how for many years he seemed a stranger to me, how I felt like we were intruders in his life.

Growing up in Oklahoma further clouded this past. I was too immersed in white America to focus on anything but the need to look and act like those around me. I was too cocooned in safety to recognize how far I had come from my prior state of need and trauma, or how close that state would always be to me.

It's only in the past few years that I've begun calling myself a refugee. I suspect my own maturation as a writer has had something to do with this. You can't write meaningfully or honestly about anything, even things that have nothing to do with your own life, if you haven't yet confronted who you are. My refugee experience does not define who I am, but for better or for worse it has informed how I see myself, how I see how others see me, and how I want to be seen.

So that begs the essential question, What *is* a refugee? It's here that I get stuck. The American version alone offers a myriad of experiences that differ vastly by country, culture, and conflict of origin; and also by time, personal as well as historical. Ask this question to a Holocaust survivor from New York, and then ask an Iranian teenager who's growing up Muslim in the South. Chances are, their answers cannot be confined to a standard definition, not to their satisfaction. Chances are, they'll tell you a story instead, and even then their stories might only capture literal experience. How do you go beyond facts and memories and get at what continues to shape the refugee long after refuge has been found? I've discovered it's more useful to ask, "What is a refugee *like*—not only to those who see her but to the refugee herself?" To this end, I have an ongoing list.

In many ways, a refugee is like an orphan. She might literally be bereft of parents, and of siblings too, but she is bereft more so of her extended family: not just grandparents, uncles, aunts, and cousins, but also the familial bonds of her homeland, her native community and culture and customs. Stripped of agency from the moment she fled that homeland and dependent now on those who can protect her, she is frequently seen as childish, no matter how old she actually is. As a result, she is pitied for what she has suffered, whether real or imagined on the part of those pitying her, and the pity will diminish the heroism of her journey and all the choices she made to survive and complete it. At the same time, as is inevitable in the act of compassion, that same pity can become a form of undue respect and admiration. People will listen to her story and sigh, offering her an exemption from judgment she might not deserve or want at all.

Like an orphan, if she's fortunate, she is adopted into a new family, but that requires an adjustment and perhaps a transformation of who she is. In many instances, in joining this new family and assuming this new identity, she will partly if not entirely forget her old ones. And on the inside, away from the eyes of those who see her only as a refugee and especially if she arrived at this status as a child, she will go on to feel as though she is not whole in some way. Her own narrative of who she is will feel incomplete because she will keep wondering where she came from, what she has lost, and what she would have become if that loss had never befallen her.

But being whole is not the refugee's sole aspiration. Wholeness suggests singularity and consistency, and the imperative of acculturation demands personal fluidity, the ability to be more than one person. Which is why a refugee is also like an actor. She knows she must assimilate in order to earn acceptance, to survive and prosper, but the act of assimilation is inevitably a performance—not of a false or superficial identity necessarily, but of one more legible to her audience. She becomes versions of herself, donning the new clothes and accessories, the new habits and modes of behavior that hew to the various settings of her new life. She must speak a different language as well as adopt a different way of talking and expressing herself. She might even change her name. Often, she is one person at home and another person at work or at school or simply in public. Her family and her people call her one name while everyone else calls her a wildly different one, though at some point she will have trouble determining which name is her true name. Over time, the new identity bleeds into the original one, or might even subsume it until what she has assimilated becomes the dominant reality of who she is. In other words, she comes to live the role that she was obliged to play, because what she's been doing this entire time is interpreting a script forced on her by the new culture or by members of her own people who already successfully performed it. Her audience will either embrace or reject her, and sometimes they'll do both simultaneously, or they will act like they embrace her while deep inside, perhaps without knowing it, they'll judge the performance insufficient.

For those who can never quite accept her, a refugee is like a ghost. To them, she's come from another world, an obscure and incomprehensible world, and now resides in the shadows of this one—an alien entity, an intruder. She can be invisible even though her presence is felt. If she is seen, she might very well be seen through, a specter both present and distant, both acknowledged and denied. She can be spoken of in whispers but also caricatured in the stories that contain her. She can be feared, even when she is not there, sometimes irrationally so, more significant and sinister than any version of herself that she could have conjured. And in that sense, she can be mythologized. She is seen as a manifestation of the past and as a dark harbinger of the future, though it can be argued that the anxiety she inspires is little more than a projection of the beholder's personal fears, deeply rooted in religious, political, and cultural beliefs that are themselves a mythos. That's all to say that a refugee's outsize effect on people, on those who cannot accept her, is motivated more often than not by the imagination. What they feel, though, is not imaginary. It is real and consequential. If anything, it is imagined into being. And that space between what is real and imaginary is ultimately where the refugee resides. Like a ghost, her state of being—to others and even to herself—is ambiguous. Her identity, her goals and desires and intentions, her place in the world she now inhabits: they are all as hazy as those memories of the world she was once born into.

These ghost-like contours of the refugee—this is what I didn't recognize until recently. I had moved on from the circumstances that brought me to America and into the life it had given me and continues to give me. But America itself never quite moves on. The country of refuge never does, regularly stirred by new conflicts that remind it of the old ones. It keeps remembering your tragic origins, no matter how successfully you've embraced and achieved the promises it originally offered. On the street, it might no longer recognize the refugee in you, but the tide of American history continually washes new versions of you onto these shores, and their shadow is your shadow too.

But why would you want America to forget? This, I suppose, is the real question I've been asking myself.

Throughout elementary school, I remember things I would say in class that would begin with the phrase, "In my country." I was referring to Vietnam, not America, and I was motivated by an innocent desire to offer my teacher and classmates exotic information. If someone mentioned an argument they'd had with their father, I would say that "in my country" you'd be spanked for talking back to an older sibling, let alone to your parents. If we were discussing the Civil War, I would say that "in my country" we'd had five or six of our own over the centuries, including the one that brought me here—something my father once told me.

What I was really doing, unknowingly, was preserving my connection to my first homeland and expressing to the class what I had lost. At an even deeper level, my need to express this was my intimation that my family and I had no choice in that loss.

By the time I got to high school, I rarely made such statements in class or anywhere else. That need was no longer there, overtaken no doubt by my successful assimilation into my second homeland. I'd become officially more *American* than *Vietnamese*, a fact my parents still mourn to this day. It wasn't out of ignorance of my Vietnamese heritage or a lack of curiosity or self-identification. It was simply a matter of time and place: I had discovered and cultivated all my desires, aversions, and beliefs here.

But then, at nineteen, I returned to Vietnam for the first time with my family. Peering through the window as our plane flew into Saigon, I felt a sudden familiarity that I found again in the heat and farraginous smells of the city, in the throng of life on the streets, in the people who at once resembled me and behaved nothing like me. For two weeks, it was the shock of recognition amid aliens, over and over.

I remember a conversation during that trip with my aunt, my mother's oldest sister, who had helped her raise me and my sister for the five years we were without our father. When we first left, she feared she would never see us again and didn't know if distance or death would be the reason. Even after our survival was confirmed, she mourned us for years and ended up naming her first daughter after my sister. She told me how stubborn and preternaturally smart my sister was back then and how people used to mistake me for a girl because of my delicate long hair. She recalled when I was two years old and my uncle—the only boy among five girls—drowned in a swimming accident. He was seventeen. I had been his constant companion, and the day after his funeral, I sat playing on the kitchen floor and sang a song he once taught me. I knew none of these things, except for his death. She recounted it all to me while smiling, a willed and hard-earned nostalgia, born from pain. In her smile, I confronted the most fundamental truth about exile: it is never yours alone. No matter how young or unaware I was when I left, I had had another life in Vietnam, and although I had moved on in America, the people from that life had never moved on from me. Even as I sat there beside my aunt as a nineteen-year-old man, the young boy I once was remained a ghost in her life, and ghosts never die.

New Lands, New Selves

NOVUYO ROSA TSHUMA

My younger sister grew up in a very different Bulawayo from mine. She is thirteen years younger, but the age difference isn't the reason hers was a different Bulawayo, rather, it was that catastrophic condition: "socio-politico-economic crisis." This socio-politico-economic crisis is what necessitated my family's move from Zimbabwe to South Africa in 2009.

Sure, hers was still the same physical Bulawayo of beautifully wide, tree-lined streets with department stores like Woolworths and Haddon & Sly—reminiscent of the British high-street shops—and businesses housed in Victorian buildings filigreed with Romanesque pillars, arches, and domes (our "gift" from the British during the epoch when they tried to "make the world in their image," a desire now taken up by America and given that stately name: Empire).

The blind man with the MC Hammer shades who, throughout my childhood, sat outside the Old Mutual Building at the corner of Eighth Avenue and Fife Street was still there, strumming his guitar and singing Don Williams songs, complete with an impressive approximation of the Texan drawl. So was the Rainbow Cinema at the Bulawayo Center along Fort Street, a haunt I used to frequent as a teenager with my friends to watch American movies and eat movie popcorn and feel cool.

The metropolitan landscape of this city of my childhood is what I cling to the most, because it remains static and unchanging, filling me with nostalgia when I visit home, unlike the family and friends I left there, who have grown and changed in ways that surprise and sadden me; we are no longer the people we used to be to one another, and we can never go back to the ease and familiarity we shared. Life has happened, to us all.

I also cling to this landscape and these memories of my childhood because they reflect my myriad experiences as a human being, something that was flattened under the Zimbabwe of the news, the Zimbabwe of the South African imagination, which conflated Zimbabweans with a narrative of perpetual crisis and suffering. This same flattening happened on a larger scale when I moved from South Africa to America in 2013 and became "African," the Africa of the Western imagination, conflating "Africans" with a narrative of perpetual crisis and suffering, so that many Americans would react to me with surprise: How come I spoke good English? How come I knew American movies and music? How had I gotten here? (I rode on an elephant until I got to the U.S. border.)

By the time my sister was born, in the year 2000, our city, our country, and our lives had begun to disintegrate, all because of Grandfather, as he is called, and his cronies; our version of the quintessential dictator, so disappointingly cliché. Sometimes I think of him as one in a series of Chucky dolls manufactured and doled out to our African (and now American) countries from the Post-Colonial Store. We bought him, we played with him, he played us, and now, here we are. But I don't want to dwell on Grandfather, the world's oldest dictator, bent, it seems, on breaking records; at ninety-three, he is still clinging to the presidency. Already, he makes purchase to so much of our mental and emotional spaces, seeking to colonize not only our bodies, but our minds as well.

Whereas I have memories of a Bulawayo childhood spent pushing overbrimming trolleys at Meikles Supermarket, spooning 4 PM yogurt snacks, gulping milk at your will, and slurping on Saturday ice cream, I imagine my sister's childhood memories are populated with those never-ending queues that decorated, from 2001 onward, our city and the rest of the country: sugar queues, cooking-oil queues, mealie-meal queues, fuel queues. Might she remember walking down Lobengula Street with Mother and I in search of the new age entrepreneurs selling rice-in-a-cup, sugar-in-a-cup, and suspicious looking fuel-in-a-bottle? Or arriving at the bank at 6 AM to find a queue already snaking like a boa constrictor down the street and, with a heavy sigh, settling down for a whole day spent in line?

Queuing became a way of life, an art form, even; you could hold your place in one queue, rush to another and hold your place there too, and, in that way, be in both at the same time. Days and itineraries had to be planned around the very important activity of queuing. Even time was measured in queues— how long a queue was, how fast it moved, how quickly one could move on to the next queue.

But how could you expect people who were hungry, scared, and very much aware that there wasn't enough for everybody to stand docilely in queues? Whenever the food trucks carrying mealie-meal (a coarse maize flour) or sugar or cooking oil were seen pulling up at the supermarkets, these queues would inevitably descend into chaos. It was all very exhilarating and, fueled by desperation, necessitated a lot of elbow shoving and body slamming. There was nothing as triumphant as emerging from a scuffle with a bag of one of these precious necessities.

Mother, ever enterprising, started a vegetable garden in our yard, our saving grace on days when there was no food in the house or no money for food. (I, a formerly middle-class kid with strict city sensibilities, became a mini–subsistence farmer.) The mother of my childhood was a professional, self-sustaining woman. She had been a mathematics teacher at Northlea High for as long as I could remember, and was loved and respected at her school. She wore her hair in a shiny perm, loved jewelry, and had a rack of expensive shoes. She had legs for days. She loved to dance, my mother did, and would often throw parties at our house. Having grown up in Lupane Village and acquired her education at a mission school, she had reinvented herself as a city woman—vivacious, fiercely independent, and possessing a zest for life.

The Bulawayo of Queues broke Mother, a little. Or maybe a lot. I could see the stress of a year, two, three, four, and then eight of the mayhem in our country, which we foolishly believed to be temporary, taking its toll. She was no longer as lively. She spent most of her time worrying. The energy she once spent loving life was now spent surviving it. The government no longer paid its civil servants, and when it did, hyperinflation was such that the whole of her monthly salary, at one point, could only buy two kilograms of chicken. She had to resort to the gritty work of entrepreneurialism: buying and selling things, trying to make a profit wherever she could, asking for donations from her sisters who had fled to the UK and Scotland. Thanks to hyperinflation, her pension became worthless—a life, a career, a future, hopes, and dreams all wiped out so very callously in the space of a few years.

Lurking so menacingly in the background of all of this were the arrests or, worse, forced disappearances of political and human rights activists, opposition party members, and civil society organizers. Very much in the foreground were the bombings of the offices of the independent newspapers, the merciless beating and jailing of any citizens who dared to come together in a political gathering, and, eventually, the beating of any citizens who dared to protest, strike, or show any form of resistance to the world Grandfather was building in his own image.

During our 2008 elections, the army generals came out on local television vowing they would never acknowledge any president other than Grandfather. Voting for the opposition was akin to voting for war, they said. And then one of them did the strangest thing: He smiled, flashing his wide, straight teeth at the camera, and encouraged Zimbabweans to go out and exercise their democratic right to vote. And then their faces disappeared from the screen, leaving us agape.

I hated Grandfather for what he was doing to us. I hate him for what he has done to us still.

· · ·

With what eagerness, then, did I embrace our move, in 2009, to South Africa? Standing in a ShopRite supermarket a day after my arrival, I gaped at a batch of bread stacked in the pastry section, hot and steamy from the oven, with that yeasty aroma that makes you want to bite off a chunk and chew greedily, savoring the warm freshness. I stared and stared at the loaves of bread, clenched and unclenched my hands, and fought the reflex to grab as much as I could and take it home to hoard. I had to remind myself that the bread would still be on the shelves the following day, and the day after, and the day after that, too. The shops would not run out of food. This was South Africa, our Africa's United States of America, where many a persecuted migrant flocked from other parts of the continent to seek refuge and enjoy the fruits of the melting pot, its love for human rights, and its relatively flourishing economy.

Now, to *dis*place a person is almost akin to *mis*placing them, denoting being moved or moving from your *proper* place, being *out of position*. There was always a sense of not being in one's *proper place* in South Africa, made clear by the stringent laws against us, *foreign objects*. I learned I was Zimbabwean in South Africa, a concept of home I hadn't grappled with before, because I had been in my homeland, feeling at home. Weddings, birthdays, parties, arguments, gossip, laughter, love, tastes and smells—of my mother's aromatic beef stew, of the Bulawayo spring perfuming the air with its floral scents—these mundane acts of daily living are what I associated with being at home. The food shortages and the never-ending queues had served as the unfortunate staging ground for our lives. But were still *us*, then, recognizable to ourselves and to each other.

Suddenly, in South Africa, I was no longer just me but Zimbabwean, part of a larger group called Zimbabweans who were *out of position*, not in our *proper* place, almost as bad as the Nigerians, seen as a burden to the national resources meant for the South Africans and a blight on the South African conscience. We were cast as degenerates, thieves, murderers, rapists, and drug peddlers polluting the South African spirit. We were identified as an economic threat out to steal jobs meant for South Africans.

I took great pains to try and hide my Zimbabwean-ness. When the *khombis* (public minibuses) were stopped by the police on their way to the city center, who would then proceed to scan us passengers, single out those who didn't "look South African" (the West Africans, especially, were easy prey for this, their physique and their accents giving them away) and demand to see identification, I would try and look nonchalantly out the window, my hands folded casually across my chest. If you didn't have the proper identification, you were ordered out of the khombi and into the back of a police van.

Similarly, when venturing into the Joburg City Center, I would take care to wear a shirt whose sleeves covered my smallpox and BCG vaccine scars on the right side of my arm, as this was another easy way in which we Zimbabweans were targeted by the police, and subsequently stopped and asked to produce identification, and possibly searched. This practice is reminiscent of the pass laws that were prevalent during apartheid, when Africans could be stopped by the apartheid police and asked to produce their "pass," documents that showed they had a right to be where they were, especially if they were in "white-only" areas. To be in these areas, they had to be maids or garden boys, for instance, employed by their white bosses. In our case, the implication seemed to be that our Zimbabwean-ness rendered us anomalies in these "South-African" areas, a notion of nation and belonging that is challenged by the diverse lives from all over the continent that make up the space that is South Africa.

Most terrifying of all have been the xenophobic rituals which have occurred, like clockwork, every few years, evoking terrifying images of the purging in slums such as Diepsloot and Khayelitsha of *foreign objects*: the beating and burning of those "alien bodies" existing outside the protection of the community of true "South Africans," egged on by feverish demands that these *kwerekweres*, these foreigners, return to their *proper places*:

The mob is patient, its feet going thud thud thud, without urgency without panic, thud thud thud, its lips spitting down with the kwerekweres down with the foreigners down with the thieving sonofabitches down down down (viva ANC viva! Amandla ngawethu, Power to the People!).

There is Saluman, there there there, can you see him? Jolly Saluman, Saluman the wife-basher. Did you hear what they did to the foreigners in Diepsloot? Did you hear what they did to the Zimbabweans the Mozambicans the Congolese in Khayelitsha? Saluman heard. He heard and he knows, that's why he's crouching behind his own wares in his own shanty, shitting himself. He knows, as it sweeps into his spaza shop, the mob, like a Sahara storm, upsets his wares and picks him up and hurls him out into the dirt path, like tumbleweed.

He's weeping, weeping already as they set his shop alight. He's not even fighting. He's become a limp rag doll as they pick him up, tumbleweed Saluman, and fling him into the fire. They lap him up greedily, the flames, and oh there he is dancing, dancing and dancing and dancing, and screaming shrilly, like he's singing.

It's through capturing moments and telling stories, such as the passage above I wrote several years ago in a fraught state during a spate of xenophobic attacks in South Africa, that we can try to understand ourselves and our new landscapes beyond the flattened news versions of ourselves. In this way, we may extend our notions of community by trying to *see* those who have been expelled from our communal imaginings, our communal humanness. Deaths such as that of twenty-six-year-old Farai Kujirichita, whose bludgeoning at the hands of a xenophobic mob in Diepsloot in Johannesburg in 2011 went viral after it was captured on video camera, are so horrifying and tragic, and bear on our psychological landscapes in ways that are terrifying, begging for a human gesture, an attempt to understand, or, at the very least, witness.

How does one, as the displaced, escape such a fate? Through chasing, maniacally, in the host country, that unstable, exclusive condition: exceptionalism. In my case, it has been through pursuing a university education and applying myself rigorously to my creative and intellectual pursuits; I was a student in South Africa, at the University of Witwatersrand, where I earned a bachelor of commerce in economics and finance. Even now, living as an immigrant in America, where I came to through a notion of "exceptionalism" (I was granted a prestigious fellowship, thanks to my creative writing, to pursue an MFA at the preeminent Iowa Writers' Workshop), I am ever working, overworking, because I'm aware of the potential, as a non-white body and passport holder from "Africa," without the safety of "being at home," of my easy disposal from the political imagination of the world. The suffering of non-white bodies is so naturalized, so overwhelming, and so ordinary that it ceases to be exceptional.

Thus, the price for escaping that ever-threatening potential of being reduced, under the glare of the sovereign power of the host country, to a mere biological fact of life, is a tireless pursuit of exceptionalism. It is an implicit understanding that only through this exceptionalism can one "earn" one's place in the new society, earn one's right to the humanity which, for those in their *proper place*, is normal. Exceptionalism, then, is really an aspiration toward safety, human rights, access to food, to water, to resources, to an edifying life, to the free pursuit of one's endeavors, to support from the state.

Those, then, who commit the crime of being deemed ordinary or mediocre pay the price of being denied entry into host countries, rendered "stuck" in the nightmares of their homelands, or given entry only under the barest of conditions—facing the glare of the "bare life," to quote philosopher Giorgio Agamben, where their existence is nothing more than a biological fact.

And yet, the sovereign does not and cannot have an all-encompassing power over human life. It cannot account, in the case of South Africa, for all those myriad Zimbabwean lives lived between the folds of national identities and state surveillance. It cannot obliterate their human face:

> . . . *a police truck rolls slowly past and the vendor squatting next to you is scooping up sweets and cigarettes and burnt scones with one hand, and her toddler with the other. You hear her shout and the surprise of it slaps your face when you hear the Ndebele dialect and realise, yet again, that this person, too, is Zimbabwean. You watch her for a moment,*

cringe at the way the toddler is dangling from her grip.
Your eyes meet. You want to say something even though
you don't know what it is you will say. Something that will
tighten the ties that already bind you. Something that can
obliterate the alarm riddling her face.

This passage is from "You in Paradise," in my story collection, *Shadows*. The scene bloomed from an incident I saw while standing at a street corner in Joburg City Center that stayed with me. I wondered about that woman; who was she beyond my flitting glimpse of her caught in the sovereign glare, fleeing the police while I stood frozen, not sure whether I, too, should run; run to where, and run why?

. . .

Our move to South Africa seemed to tire Mother. My family moved to a small town called Piet Retief, in the Mpumalanga province of South Africa. There, Mother found work as a primary school teacher in a private school, where her knowledge of high school mathematics was of no use, and where she accumulated no pension, because of her status as a foreigner.

Just like our different Bulawayos, my younger sister probably knows a different mother than the one I grew up with. The mother I remember used to take me to the Bulawayo Drive-In to watch movies like *Honey I Blew Up the Kid* and on trips to Botswana to visit her swanky friends. My younger sister's mother—*our* mother—has taken to a new love for church and the bible. She no longer hosts parties, has made no real effort at building meaningful friendships in Piet Retief, and, unlike her teaching days at Northlea High, finds little joy in her job.

She is always dreaming of home, not the home of Grandfather's imagining and design, but another home, probably the
home our countrymen dreamed of when we attained independence from Britain in 1980.

She has gone through various displacements in her life.
Perhaps that is why she is so tired. She was in her early teens
when our liberation war with the colonial state of Rhodesia
broke out in the 1970s, and had to go into hiding in the bush
in her village. She also lived through another terrifying period
of upheaval in our country, Gukurahundi, the state genocide
of some twenty thousand civilians in the Matabeleland region
which took place right after our independence in 1980. She has
refused to speak about this period, save for her experiences at
Dukwi Refugee Camp in Botswana, where she and her siblings
fled to during the time of the genocide.

She was surprisingly animated when she told me about
fleeing to the refugee camp, fixating on a particular memory:
a female guard at the camp who was like a mother to her, who
took care, one time, to reserve a lovely, turquoise dress with a
lace collar for her from the donations that arrived at the camp,
newer and more glamorous than the other clothes. Mother's
eyes sparkled when she talked about that dress, and I can imagine how, to a young girl in her early twenties stuck in the dry
Kalahari landscape in that refugee camp, that dress, its dazzling
colors, its newness, and the very fact that it had been picked out
especially for her, must have been a very special thing.

Perhaps it's these small, precious moments within the gray,
larger canvas of suffering—within the upheavals, the displacements, the pain, the disappointing discovery of the ordinariness
of it all for people who look like us—that shine through in the

aftermath of it all, and serve as a basis for moving on, for living. In our selective arranging of memory, we may find ourselves leaning more toward light and lightheartedness. A yearning for happiness, for tenderness. An attempt to displace heartache and pain.

In 2013, after I had been admitted to the hospital in Iowa City because I was feeling *unreal*—the landscape felt unreal and kept wriggling before my eyes, and my hands kept dislodging at the wrists from the rest of my body—doctors suggested that I was suffering from post-traumatic stress disorder because of the "terrible time" I had gone through in Zimbabwe. I threw back my head and laughed. I couldn't help it. And though that time *was* terrible, I had never thought it exceptional; ours had been a suffering on a national scale, so widespread as to feel "normal." This was not the kind of exceptionalism I aspired toward, the exceptionalism of having suffered through something in my home country that I thought I had conquered by leaving, but that now seemed to have somehow found its way into my bags and my new life and was now attempting to conquer me psychologically.

"It was hard for everybody, you know," Noma, a character from my strangely similar short story "Doctor S" in *Shadows* (written before my move to Iowa City), tells her psychiatrist. "And you know, Zimbabweans are the most resilient people in the world . . . You just had to be strong with everybody else . . . you can't just choose to be special . . ."

The kind of exceptionalism I was aspiring toward, however, alienated me from my past and the people I had left at home. When I visited home in 2015, I was surprised by how much my Bulawayo had changed. The Rainbow Cinema, that haunt of my teens, had closed down. The blind man with the MC Hammer shades was still there, thankfully, his presence tethering me to a nostalgic sense of the past; I remember rushing past him, in my teens, on way to the City Hall to catch the school bus, the winter air slapping my Vaselined cheeks, making my teeth chatter. Sometimes I would drop some money into his tin can. Sometimes I wouldn't even notice him. Now, I think about him.

Sitting at Haefelis Café with some friends, another favorite old spot that had been quite fancy in my teens, I complained about the fall in standards, how ridiculous it was that we were being served orange juice in dainty coffee cups because the café said it was out of glasses.

"Eh," I lamented loudly. "Grandfather has really done us in. We can't even afford proper glasses anymore! Why the hell is he still in power? When will we kick him out?"

The table went quiet. And then, one by one, some of my friends said they had to go, and stood up and left.

"You shouldn't say that," said one of my friends who stayed behind. "Why are you drawing attention to yourself by talking about Grandfather?"

"What did I say?" I asked, shrugging. "I didn't say anything. I only said—"

"*Shoosh!* You never know who may be listening. Even among us, you never know who may be an informant."

I threw back my head and laughed. "One of our friends, an informant? Come, now."

Frowning, visibly irritated, my friend clutched my hand and said, "Don't act like you never lived here."

I stopped laughing. Had it really been like this, in my teens? I blinked repeatedly, trying to remember. The ground beneath me suddenly felt like quicksand, into which the old pieces of me I had been clinging to were rapidly disappearing.

Though I still yearn for "home," I no longer think of it as a place out there, to go to. It now resides in me, a "feeling at home" inside of me that I try to cultivate every day, that I can take with me wherever I need to go.

Refugee Children: The Yang Warriors

KAO KALIA YANG

The kids watched Chinese historical dramas dubbed in Thai in the refugee camp's one-baht movie house, a darkened shack with a dirt floor where a twenty-inch television was propped on a high shelf. Then, they practiced.

In our compound, the Yang Clan, the children chose a master. After much thought and deliberation, they chose by unanimous vote a cousin named Mc. His name translated into "little." He was a little guy, even by refugee camp standards. He was about ten years old at the time. He had a bit of a potbelly, round and hard, a tiny hill on the flat expanse of his thin body. The children said they chose him as their leader not because he was the oldest, or the biggest, or the smartest, but because he cared the most. They wanted their leader to be someone who would leave none of them behind in the event of a battle to the death.

The adults asked what battles they were anticipating. The children shrugged their shoulders. It was better to be trained and ready than to be caught unaware and die unremarkably. There were enemies everywhere in that place we shared: the camp guards with their guns, the other refugee children who were often territorial over play space, and the endless supply of ghosts. People died all the time in the camp, the old ones, the young ones, the sick ones, even the healthy ones. In each part of the compound, there were stories of the dead returning, often because they knew one day we would be leaving the camp behind and they were lonely and wanted friends.

There were ten children in the group. The older cousins who had not been elected as the master did not want to participate. So, it was mostly a group of ten and under, eight boys and two girls. In the gray dawn before the hot sun made its mark across the wide skies, Master Me drew lines in the dirt of the compound. Before the adults and most of the children in the compound were up, the disciples would be on their lines ready to begin the training of the day. In the mornings, they balanced rocks on their heads. They did not stop until they were called in for lunch. After lunch, they practiced drills using long sticks they found across the expanse of the refugee camp. They used the sticks like magical swords, and did moves balancing on one foot and then the other. Once in a while, they did mental battles against each other so their minds could stay as sharp as their bodies. The kids stood in a circle around the fighting pair, silent and respectful. The "demonstrators"—as they were called—took turns bowing and then sitting down for the matches. They'd sit cross-legged on the ground across from each other, eyes closed, and hold their hands in front of their small bodies like a Thai greeting, except far more rigid in posture. They breathed in through their noses with brows furrowed. They did not move for hours. Beneath the hot sun, they sat in pools of sweat—while the "observers" kept the hungry dogs and chickens away from them. Sometimes, the matches took an hour or more. In the end, the victor was the person who had the greatest focus and fortitude, the one who could concentrate the longest in position. Over time, a hierarchy formed in the group, from Master Me down. The youngest in the group, a little girl no older than five, was the least formidable, thus, most vulnerable member. Everyone's job was to look out for her.

Occasionally, the group took on special missions. One particularly hot week when the camp rations were thin, Master Me decided that his contingent would make an excursion out of the camp to go and forage for morning glory. There was a big rule in the camp: no Hmong person could leave without written permission. We had all seen men and women beaten to the brink of death for leaving the camp. We all knew of individuals who had simply disappeared after reports of them leaving the camp were filed by the authorities, Thai men with guns. It was a dangerous proposition. Still, after a long day of meditation, it came upon Master Me that his group could provide good, healthy greens to the young children of the compound by secretly leaving the camp and finding food. He told his group that if they were caught by the authorities or the adults, then he would fulfill his destiny as their chosen leader by standing for all administered consequences.

I was five years old but my playground was the reach of my mother's skirt, so I was not a member of the group. My older sister Dawb was. She was one of the two girls. She was seven years old at the time. She'd had polio as a baby so one of her legs was shorter than the other. She walked with a limp. Away from our mother and father's hearing, everyone, including adults, called her the handicapped one. She'd been granted membership in the group because she was willing to carry the flip-flops of other group members whenever they were on the run from the animals or the other refugee children who chased them. Although not fast or strong, she was good at the mental battles. I knew about the excursion through my sister.

The night before the big outing, Dawb could not sleep. She tossed and turned in the hot night. When our mother had turned to the wall and our father's snores grew steady, she whispered in my ear, "Tomorrow might be my last day."

I was agitated by her restlessness. The drama of her statement did little to pique my interest.

I told Dawb in a whisper, "Stop talking. Go to sleep."

Her voice, when she spoke again, was very serious. She said, "Tomorrow, we are going to go look for food."

I interrupted her, "For rats again?"

She said, "No, this time it is going to be more dangerous. We are leaving the camp."

I couldn't find enough air in the room to breathe out my words, "You can't."

Dawb shushed me and explained, "Master Me has meditated on this for a full day. He believes it is our only way to save you and the younger children in the compound. You haven't had greens for days."

I said, "I don't even like greens. You're not supposed to go out of the camp. None of us are. If our mother and father knew, you'd be in trouble. Grandma would take a stick to your behind. The authorities would kill you."

She said, "I know all that. I'm telling you this so that if we don't come back tomorrow, you can tell Mom and Dad where we've gone. Master Me already went on a secret scouting mission. He knows that not far from here, there's a farm. The farmers have a pond. It is full of morning glory. Tomorrow morning, at first light, we are setting out. Our plan is to be back before lunch."

Dawb took a few deep breaths and then fell asleep. I looked at the shadows across our sleeping chamber, saw the moonlit shadows grow thick and then thin.

By the time, I woke up the next morning, Dawb was gone. My mother had left to tend to her small garden behind the sewage canal, a dry patch with rows of cilantro and green onions, which she harvested and sold in small bunches by the road into the camp. My father, too, was gone. He was likely carrying water from the well. I looked at my sister's place beside me and I knew my sister was not out in the compound yard, standing at her line, balancing rocks on her head. I felt a queasiness grow in my stomach. I got up and went about my morning routine, biting my lip each time I saw an adult, looking left and right across the spread of my cousins, making note of the missing people, not quite believing that their absence wasn't registering. At some point during mid-morning, one of my aunties got mad after she couldn't find one of my cousins, a member of the group. She said, "I'm going to wring his neck when he comes back, disappearing all morning to catch tadpoles."

I sat and watched my mother and my aunts cook lunch from my woven bamboo stool. I held my arms across my queasy belly. The women moved gracefully about the three or four cement stoves, little cement buckets carrying red embers and open flame. They were all thin because we didn't have much food in the camp. The first priority was always the children. In their Thai sarongs with their long black hair clipped back in buns, they looked like a movie image I'd once seen at the one-baht movie house. I thought about the death scenes of the historical Chinese dramas. Once the big battles were fought, horses, men, and women scattered about the landscape, piles of bodies, bleeding and still. Fallen flags drowned in pools of blood. I was about to get up to go and tell my mother about the probable demise of my sister, when I saw the five-year-old girl enter the doorway of the cooking area. She was soaking wet and she carried a big plastic bag of greens in her hands. She left it quietly by the doorway. Before the adults saw her, she left. I followed her quickly.

"Ib, where's Dawb?" I asked.

She said, "Hurt."

I felt the tears burning.

I said, "Where is she?"

She said, "Behind the corn husk shack. She was not the only one injured."

The two of us ran our way to the corn husk shack. I didn't know what to expect. Perhaps one of her arms or legs had been cut off? Maybe, she'd suffered a deadly blow to the stomach or the head? My heart was pounding with each step.

When we finally made it to the corn shack, I saw the group. My sister was lying on Master Me's lap. Her forehead was bleeding. A deep cut across the side of her temple. Another cousin was also lying down. His bleeding foot was in the arms of another cousin who was trying to wrap an old shirt around it.

Before I knew it, someone yelled, "Grandma's coming!"

The scattering was amazing.

By the time I made out the sound of my grandma's key chains rattling with her unsteady walk, only the injured parties were left with Master Me before them.

Once Grandma arrived on the scene, the rest of the adults arrived as well. Most of the group members had been caught, their mothers and fathers holding them by the arms and shirts like common thieves. They were all soaking wet from the venture into the pond. There wasn't much talk (no one wanted to draw the attention of the Thai authorities), but there was a switch and it flew into butts, whimpers and yelps caught in frightened throats. Master Me took the heaviest of the whippings. I remember an adult voice whispering harshly, "You could have killed everyone."

For lunch, I ate fried morning glory that day. It was fried with garlic and seasoned with fish sauce. I ate it with broken rice on a white metal plate with peeling enamel. I had never liked greens, but I remember the crunch of the morning glory stalks and how the oil had seasoned my rice, made it slippery, slightly sweet from the garlic. I ate it with the other younger children from the compound at the long table. None of the members ate the morning glory meal with us. They chose not to on their own accord. They understood that it was their honor at stake. They looked over us as we cleared our plates and licked our spoons, hungrier than even we knew for the taste of wild greens, a hint of freedom from beyond the fenced compound we knew as home.

They had been mere children before the meal, playing a game I was not particularly interested in, but after that morning glory meal, they became the warriors of my childhood in Ban Vinai Refugee Camp. We'd all heard the stories of how our mothers and fathers and our grandmother went through a war in Laos to bring us to Thailand. I knew we were survivors. I had not imagined us as warriors.

Long before we left that dry, dusty, hungry place, it was they who taught us how to venture beyond our captivity.

I see them now from the far distance of time and space, a group of ten children, standing on their dirt lines beneath the bright sun. At their center was Master Me, a potbellied boy who stood without a shirt, his skin glistening with sweat, his shorts falling well beyond his knees, in the bright sunshine, spine straight, gazing not at the world around us but within himself. I see at the edge of the circle the two girls, the five-year-old frowning away her discomfort, growing taller than her years, and my older sister Dawb, with her scar across her left temple, one of her legs slightly shorter than the other, braced against the earth. They are glorious in the sun of my youth, warriors standing for all of us.

List of Contributors

Joseph Azam—Born in Afghanistan, Joseph Azam moved with his family to the United States as a young boy. Azam is an attorney focused on internal investigations and global anticorruption. He is currently senior vice president and chief compliance and ethics officer at Infor; is on the Board of Governors at the University of California, Hastings College of Law; and is a member of the Organizing Committee for the Afghan-American Conference, an annual conference that brings together members of the Afghan diaspora in the United States. He has written for a number of publications, including *Lucky Peach* and the *San Francisco Chronicle*. He lives in New York City.

Chris Abani is a novelist, poet, essayist, screenwriter, and playwright. Born in Nigeria to an Igbo father and English mother, he grew up in Afikpo, Nigeria, received a BA in English from Imo State University, Nigeria, an MA in English, Gender and Culture from Birkbeck College, University of London, and a PhD in Literature and Creative Writing from the University of Southern California. He has resided in the United States since 2001. He is the recipient of the PEN USA Freedom-to-Write Award, the Prince Claus Award, a Lannan Literary Fellowship, a California Book Award, a Hurston/Wright Legacy Award, a PEN Beyond the Margins Award, the PEN Hemingway Book Prize, and a Guggenheim Award. His fiction includes *The Secret*

History of Las Vegas and *Song for Night.* His poetry collections include *Sanctificum* and *There Are No Names for Red.* Abani is known as an international voice on humanitarianism, art, ethics, and our shared political responsibility. He is Board of Trustees Professor of English at Northwestern University.

David Bezmozgis is the author of *Natasha and Other Stories, The Free World,* and *The Betrayers.* He has also written and directed two feature films, *Victoria Day* and *Natasha.* He lives in Toronto, where he is the director of the Humber School for Writers.

Fatima Bhutto was born in Kabul, grew up in Damascus, and lives in Karachi. She is the author of several books, including most recently *Songs of Blood and Sword* (Nation Books, 2010) and *The Shadow of the Crescent Moon* (Penguin, 2014). Her work has appeared in the *Guardian,* the *Financial Times,* and *Granta,* among other places.

Thi Bui was born in Việt Nam and came to the United States in 1978 as part of the "boat people" wave of refugees from Southeast Asia fleeing the aftermath of war. Her debut graphic memoir, *The Best We Could Do,* has been selected as UCLA's Common Book for 2017–18 and featured on several Best of 2017 lists, such as the *Washington Post* and *Booklist.* She is the illustrator of *A Different Pond,* a critically acclaimed children's book by Bao Phi. Her short comics can be found online at *The Nib* and PEN America. Thi taught high school in New York City and was a founding teacher of Oakland International High School, the first public high school in California for recent immigrants and English learners. She currently teaches in the MFA in Comics program at the California College of the Arts and is working on a graphic nonfiction narrative about climate change in the Mê Kông Delta.

Ariel Dorfman, a Chilean-American author whose plays (among them, *Death and the Maiden*) have been performed in over one hundred countries, has written numerous award-winning books (novels, stories, poems, memoirs, essays) that have been translated and published in more than sixty languages. Accompanied by his wife Angélica, Ariel divides his time between Chile and the United States, where he is professor emeritus of literature at Duke University. A regular contributor to the *New York Times* and many major newspapers worldwide, his most recent books are a collection of essays, *Homeland Security Ate My Speech*, and the novel *Darwin's Ghosts*.

Lev Golinkin is the author of *A Backpack, a Bear, and Eight Crates of Vodka*, Amazon's Debut of the Month, a Barnes & Noble Discover Great New Writers program selection, and winner of the Premio Salerno Libro d'Europa. Mr. Golinkin, a graduate of Boston College, came to the United States as a child refugee from the eastern Ukrainian city of Kharkov (now called Kharkiv) in 1990. His writing on the Ukraine crisis, Russia, the far right, and immigrant and refugee identity has appeared in the *New York Times*, the *Washington Post*, the *Los Angeles Times*, CNN, the *Boston Globe*, *Politico Europe*, and Time.com, among other publications; he has been interviewed by NPR, ABC Radio, WSJ Live, and HuffPost Live.

Reyna Grande—Born in Iguala, Guerrero, Mexico, Reyna was two years old when her father left for the United States to find work. Her mother followed her father north two years later, leaving Reyna and her siblings behind in Mexico. In 1985, when Reyna was going on ten, she left Iguala and entered the United States as an undocumented immigrant, and later went on to become the first person in her family to graduate from college. Now, she is an award-winning novelist and memoirist. She has received an American Book Award, the El Premio Aztlán Literary Award, and the International Latino Book Award. In 2012, she was a finalist for the prestigious National Book Critics Circle Awards, and in 2015 she was honored with a Luis Leal Award for Distinction in Chicano/Latino Literature. Her novels, *Across a Hundred Mountains* and *Dancing with Butterflies*, were published to critical acclaim. In her latest book, *The Distance Between Us*, Reyna writes about her life before and after immigrating as a child from Mexico to the United States. It is now available as a young readers edition from Aladdin Books. Her new memoir, *A Dream Called Home*, will be published in 2018 by Atria.

Meron Hadero was born in Addis Ababa, Ethiopia, and lived in Germany before arriving in the United States as a refugee. She has been published in *Best American Short Stories*, *Selected Shorts* on NPR/PRI, the *Missouri Review*, *Boulevard*, *The Offing*, *Indiana Review*, *The Normal School*, and *Addis Ababa Noir*. Her essays have appeared in the *New York Times Book Review* and *Off Assignment*. She has been a fellow at the MacDowell Colony, Yaddo, and Ragdale, and she has received grants from the NEA, the International Institute at the University of Michigan, the Elizabeth George Foundation, and Artist Trust. Meron worked at the Bill & Melinda Gates Foundation and is a former World Affairs Council fellow in Seattle. She holds an MFA in creative writing from the Helen Zell Writers' Program at the University of Michigan, a JD from Yale Law School, and an AB from Princeton University in history with a certificate in American studies. She lives in Oakland and is a member of the San Francisco Writers' Grotto.

Aleksandar Hemon—Born in Sarajevo, Aleksandar Hemon was visiting Chicago in 1992, intending to stay for a few months, until his hometown came under siege and he was unable to return. He is the author of *The Lazarus Project*, which was a finalist for the National Book Award and the National Book Critics Circle Award, and three collections of short stories. He is the recipient of a Guggenheim Fellowship and a "genius grant" from the MacArthur Foundation. He lives in Chicago.

Joseph Kertes—Born in Hungary, Joseph Kertes and his family escaped to Canada after the revolution of 1956. Kertes founded the creative writing program at Humber College, and for fifteen years he was Dean of Creative and Performing Arts. He is the author of four novels for adults, including *Gratitude*, which won the Jewish Book Award for Fiction, and two books for children. His latest novel, inspired by his own experience as a refugee, is called *The Afterlife of Stars*. He lives in Toronto, Canada.

Porochista Khakpour is the author of the memoir *Sick* and the novels *The Last Illusion* (a 2014 "Best Book of the Year" according to NPR, *Kirkus Reviews*, BuzzFeed, *PopMatters*, Electric Literature, and more) and *Sons and Other Flammable Objects* (the

2007 California Book Award winner in "First Fiction," a *Chicago Tribune* "Fall's Best," and a *New York Times* "Editor's Choice"). Her writing has appeared in the *New York Times,* the *Los Angeles Times,* the *Wall Street Journal, Al Jazeera America, Bookforum, Slate, Salon, Spin,* CNN, the *Daily Beast, Elle,* and many other publications around the world. She's had fellowships from the National Endowment for the Arts, the University of Leipzig (Picador Guest Professorship), Yaddo, Ucross, and Northwestern University's Academy for Alternative Journalism, among others. She was last writer-in-residence at Bard College, adjunct faculty at Columbia University, and visiting faculty at VCFA's MFA program. Born in Tehran and raised in the Los Angeles area, she lives in New York City's Harlem.

Marina Lewycka was born in a refugee camp in Germany in 1946, of Ukrainian parents who had been taken there as forced laborers during World War II. She grew up in England, lived mostly in Yorkshire, and worked as a teacher and lecturer. She started writing when she was four years old, but published her best-selling comedic novel *A Short History of Tractors in Ukrainian* when she was fifty-seven. She has since published four more novels, of which the latest, *The Lubetkin Legacy,* was nominated for the Bollinger/Everyman/Wodehouse Prize for comic fiction.

Maaza Mengiste is a novelist and essayist. Her debut novel, *Beneath the Lion's Gaze,* was selected by the *Guardian* as one of the ten best contemporary African books and named one of the best books of 2010 by *Christian Science Monitor, Boston Globe,* and other publications. She is a Fulbright Scholar and has received fellowships from the National Endowment for the Arts, Yaddo, the Virginia Center for the Creative Arts, and Northwestern University's Center for the Writing Arts, among other places. Her work can be found in the *New Yorker, Granta,* the *Guardian,* the *New York Times, Rolling Stone,* BBC Radio, the *New Inquiry,* and *Lettre International,* among other places. She was a writer on the documentary projects *Girl Rising* and *The Invisible City: Kakuma.* Her second novel is forthcoming.

Dina Nayeri's second novel, *Refuge,* was published by Riverhead Books in July 2017. She is the winner of an O. Henry Prize and a National Endowment for the Arts literature grant, and fellowships from the MacDowell Colony, Bogliasco Foundation, and others. Her writing has appeared in the *Guardian,* the *New York Times,* the *Los Angeles Times, Wall Street Journal, Vice,* and many other publications and has been translated to fourteen languages. She holds an MFA from the Iowa Writers' Workshop and an MBA from Harvard. She is currently adapting the essay included here, "The Ungrateful Refugee," into a book of narrative nonfiction on the refugee life, coming from Canongate Books in 2019.

Raja Shehadeh is a writer and lawyer. His books include *Strangers in the House; Language of Peace, Language of War: Palestine, Israel and the Search for Justice; Palestinian Walks: Notes on a Vanishing Landscape,* for which he won the 2008 Orwell Prize for Political Writing; and *A Rift in Time: Travels with My Ottoman Uncle.* Shehadeh is a founder of the pioneering human rights organization Al Haq, an affiliate of the International Commission of Jurists. His most recent book is *Where the Line* *is Drawn: A Tale of Crossings, Friendships, and Fifty Years of Occupation in Israel-Palestine.*

Vu Tran was born in Saigon, Vietnam, and raised in Oklahoma. He is the winner of a Whiting Award, and his short stories have appeared in many publications, including the *O. Henry Prize Stories* and the *Best American Mystery Stories*. His first novel, *Dragonfish*, was a *New York Times* Notable Book. He is currently an assistant professor of practice in english and creative writing at the University of Chicago, where he directs the fiction program.

Novuyo Rosa Tshuma is a writer from Zimbabwe. In 2009, her family had to leave Zimbabwe for South Africa, one amongst millions of Zimbabwean families who have fled their homeland in search of better living conditions in the neighboring country. Her novella and short story collection, *Shadows*, which chronicles the lives of Zimbabweans living both in Zimbabwe and South Africa, was published to critical acclaim in 2013 by the South African publisher Kwela and awarded the 2014 Herman Charles Bosman Prize. Novuyo is a graduate of the Iowa Writers' Workshop, and has received fellowships from the Kimmel Harding Nelson Center for the Arts and Inprint, as well as a prestigious Bellagio Literary Arts Residency Award from the Rockefeller Foundation for her novel *House of Stone*. Novuyo serves on the Editorial Advisory Board of the *Bare Life Review*, a journal of refugee and immigrant literature based in New York.

Kao Kalia Yang is a Hmong American writer. She is the author of *The Latehomecomer: A Hmong Family Memoir* (Coffee House Press, 2008), winner of the 2009 Minnesota Book Awards in Creative Nonfiction/Memoir and Readers Choice, and a finalist for the PEN USA Award in Creative Nonfiction and the Asian Literary Award in Nonfiction. Her second book, *The Song Poet* (Metropolitan Books, 2016), won the 2016 Minnesota Book Award in Creative Nonfiction/Memoir. It was a finalist for the National Book Critics Circle Award, the Chautauqua Prize, a PEN USA Award in Nonfiction, and the Dayton's Literary Peace Prize. Yang is also a teacher and a public speaker.

THE DISPLACED